CAMBRIDGE   MUSIC   HANDBOOKS

Strauss: *Also sprach Zarathustra*

Donated to
Augustana
University College
by
Augustana's
Students' Union
Capital Development Fund
2001-2004

CAMBRIDGE MUSIC HANDBOOKS

GENERAL EDITOR Julian Rushton

Cambridge Music Handbooks provide accessible introductions to major musical works, written by the most informed commentators in the field.

With the concert-goer, performer and student in mind, the books present essential information on the historical and musical context, the composition, and the performance and reception history of each work, or group of works, as well as critical discussion of the music.

Other published titles

Bach: Mass in B Minor JOHN BUTT
Beethoven: *Missa solemnis* WILLIAM DRABKIN
Beethoven: Symphony No. 9 NICHOLAS COOK
Berg: Violin Concerto ANTHONY POPLE
Chopin: The Four Ballades JIM SAMSON
Handel: *Messiah* DONALD BURROWS
Haydn: *The Creation* NICHOLAS TEMPERLEY
Haydn: String Quartets, Op. 50 W. DEAN SUTCLIFFE
Janáček: *Glagolitic Mass* PAUL WINGFIELD
Mahler: Symphony No. 3 PETER FRANKLIN
Musorgsky: *Pictures at an Exhibition* MICHAEL RUSS
Schoenberg: *Pierrot lunaire* JONATHAN DUNSBY
Schubert: *Die schöne Müllerin* SUSAN YOUENS
Schumann: Fantasie, Op. 17 NICHOLAS MARSTON
Sibelius: Symphony No. 5 JAMES HEPOKOSKI

Strauss: *Also sprach Zarathustra*

John Williamson
University of Liverpool

Published by the Press Syndicate of the University of Cambridge
The Pitt Building, Trumpington Street, Cambridge CB2 1RP
40 West 20th Street, New York, NY 10011–4211, USA
10 Stamford Road, Oakleigh, Melbourne 3166, Australia

First published 1993

Printed in Great Britain at the University Press, Cambridge

A cataloguing in publication record for this book is available from the British Library

Library of Congress cataloguing in publication data
Williamson, John.
Strauss: Also sprach Zarathustra / John Williamson
p. cm. – (Cambridge music handbooks)
Includes bibliographical references and index.
ISBN 0 521 40076 7. – ISBN 0 521 40935 7 (pbk)
1. Strauss, Richard, 1864–1949. Also sprach Zarathustra.
I. Title. II. Series.
ML410.S93W55 1993
784.2'184–dc20 92–20457 CIP MN

ISBN 0 521 40076 7 hardback
ISBN 0 521 40935 7 paperback

AH

for Roger and Eleanor

Contents

Contents

Acknowledgements

At least one reviewer of earlier titles in this series has claimed that it is specifically devoted to 'musical masterpieces'. *Also sprach Zarathustra* may sit a little awkwardly in such company, since its mastery is hardly uncontested; nor is it necessarily the most popular of Strauss's tone poems. A handbook about it runs the risk of being at least as much a study of a 'case' as of a masterpiece. I have not avoided the former aspect, for *Zarathustra* has its place in several discussions, about programme music, about theories of form, and about the nature of tonality in the late nineteenth century. Perhaps when such debates are finally understood in their full complexity, the 'mastery' of *Zarathustra* will be settled one way or the other. That it is of great importance in Strauss's development is hardly to be questioned. Ultimately, *Zarathustra* seems worthy of study for its place in the whole area of 'words and music', and for the manner in which it has overcome critical hostility to win new audiences in the last quarter of a century.

Of the various people who have contributed to this book, I should like to thank Dr Franz Trenner and Dr Robert Münster of the Bayerische Staatsbibliothek, who made it possible for me to examine photocopies of Strauss's sketches for *Zarathustra*. Dr Eveline Nikkels kindly sent me a copy of an as yet unpublished article on Strauss and Nietzsche. Julian Rushton provided numerous valuable suggestions and encouragements, and Penny Souster also was invaluable in urging me on to complete the book. Traditionally at this point one thanks also one's family; in the present case two of them insisted that the book be dedicated to them.

Abbreviations

References to Nietzsche's *Also sprach Zarathustra* in translation are always to *Thus Spoke Zarathustra: A Book for Everyone and No One*, trans. R. J. Hollingdale (rev. edn, Harmondsworth: Penguin, 1969).

The following abbreviations are used in referring to Nietzsche's work in translation:

FW (= *Die fröhliche Wissenschaft*) *The Gay Science*, trans. Walter Kaufmann (New York: Vintage, 1974).

EH (= *Ecce Homo*) *On the Genealogy of Morals* and *Ecce Homo*, trans. Walter Kaufmann and R. J. Hollingdale (New York: Vintage, 1967).

References to pages are by Arabic numerals; references to sections or aphorisms are by Arabic numeral preceded by §.

Unless stated, all translations are my own.

1

'Freely after Nietzsche'

According to Strauss's subtitle, *Also sprach Zarathustra* is a 'tone poem freely after Nietzsche'. Any commentary on the work must start from the implications of that description. The central claim is that *Zarathustra* is in some way 'poetic', a term which in the history of nineteenth-century music had carried many resonances. By Strauss's time, music's desire to be considered poetic had hardened into at least one genre, the symphonic poem, a description invented by Liszt for the cycle of twelve single-movement orchestral pieces composed in his Weimar period. Since each of these works had a programme (whether a detailed preface, an allusive title, or a pre-existing text such as a poem), 'symphonic poetry' and programme music were usually seen as in some measure related. The Lisztian symphonic poem accordingly was sucked into the debate over programme music which involved composers, historians and aestheticians (together with the musical journalists who acted as propagandists for the various standpoints within the controversy).

Superficially, Strauss used the label 'tone poem' to distinguish himself from Liszt. He applied it to a series of one-movement works (each with stated or implied programmes) which could easily have been confused with Lisztian symphonic poems. The confusion was rendered all the more likely because of his known admiration for Liszt. When composing *Macbeth* (the first of his tone poems), Strauss spoke of it in one letter as 'a kind of symphonic poem but not after Liszt'.[1] The description tacitly admits the possibility of confusion and attempts to combat it, but cannot shake off the root of the confusion, the existence of a label, 'symphonic poem', which seems to define the work in advance. That label was never actually discarded in private, and Strauss used the description 'symphonic poem' for *Zarathustra* in his correspondence.[2] For public consumption, however, he preferred 'tone poem'. In this he may have been motivated by a certain need to be seen as going beyond Liszt, to the point that he drew a cloak over certain real aspects of his music. Equally, he may have felt that to cling to a Lisztian genre and description overlooked the important contribution made to his style by Wagnerian music drama (see chapter 2).

Ex. 1 *Also sprach Zarathustra*, bars 5–6, Nature motive

Ex. 2 bars 30–2, Longing motive

Ex. 3 bars 150–3, Disgust motive

Ex. 4 bars 35–8, Faith motive

Ex. 5 bars 251–9, Dance or Zarathustra motive

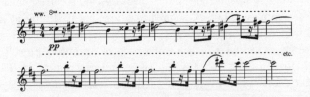

Ex. 6a bars 23–4, Dread motive

Ex. 6b bars 95–6, Life-urge motive

Ex. 6c bars 115–19, Passion motive

As a result of the influence of Wagner, early descriptions of *Also sprach Zarathustra* have a curious affinity with operatic guidebooks, particularly those that set out to identify leitmotifs and relate them to characters, concepts or places. In one of the first descriptions of *Zarathustra*, Hans Merian set forth such a list of leitmotifs with fairly clear labels. These labels have proved remarkably durable in accounts of *Zarathustra*, to the point that to discard them almost invites misunderstanding. The three main motives in this account were those of Nature (Ex. 1), Longing (Ex. 2) and Disgust (Ex. 3). To them he added others and named them in the manner of the guidebooks. The A flat hymnal melody beginning in bar 35 was the Faith theme (Ex. 4), the high B major motive from bar 251 was the Dance theme (Ex. 5).[3] The procedure proved extendable by adopting labels from Arthur Hahn's published programme for the work to produce Dread, Life-urge and Passion themes (Ex. 6). Whereas the tradition of Liszt criticism had stressed transformation of themes, writers on Strauss preferred an approach based on a conceptual identification of themes, though in practice Merian's position was rather more complex than this description implies (see chapter 7). The result was two-fold: to weaken the perception of a symphonic element in Strauss's tone poems (an element which his private letters acknowledged), and to underline a certain narrative quality in his concept of 'tone poetry'; arguably the latter went beyond the degree to which Strauss himself was committed to programme music.

The symphonic element in Liszt's genre depended in part upon the compression of the traditional movements of the symphony into sections, in part upon the retention of sonata form as an overall framework. Elements of these strategies survive clearly in the Straussian tone poem, particularly in the earliest examples, *Macbeth*, *Don Juan* and *Tod und Verklärung*. *Zarathustra* represents a rather different principle, however, which caused considerable difficulty amongst analysts. The composer-critic Hermann von Waltershausen noted that its form hardly seemed symphonic at all. Rather, it resembled a series of smaller units, the two- and three-part song-forms of German *Formenlehre* (which correspond roughly to the English binary and ternary, labels that are seldom used, however, with quite the same degree of precision as their German equivalents). In Waltershausen's interpretation, this type of structure was more suited to the kind of music drama that Strauss would later compose in *Salome*.[4] In appearing to jettison the symphonic, *Zarathustra* was not uniquely innovative, since sonata form had already been under severe stress even in such works as *Tod und Verklärung* and *Don Juan*, partly through architectonic innovation, partly through tonal departures from earlier norms. *Zarathustra*'s immediate predecessor, *Till Eulenspiegel*, had discarded sonata form completely in favour of rondo, its successor, *Don Quixote*, would adopt variation form, thus creating a triptych of works which seemed to depart formally from certain patterns of 'symphonic poetry', before Strauss returned to a more recognizably Lisztian outline in *Ein Heldenleben*.

In this can be seen a reflection of *Zarathustra*'s innovatory aspect and transitional place in the line of Strauss's tone poems. In his letters to potential conductors, Strauss had to stress several times the unusual length of the piece for a tone poem. Its duration of approximately half an hour comfortably outlasted *Tod und Verklärung*, the longest of the earlier tone poems, thus beginning the process of expansion that saw the genre move closer to, and ultimately beyond, the duration of a Brahmsian symphony, a development that indeed gradually saw the word 'symphony' reclaimed to describe, however loosely, the genre of Strauss's orchestral works (as in the *Sinfonia Domestica* and *Eine Alpensinfonie*). This sudden expansion in *Zarathustra* was matched by an increase in orchestral resources. Where some saw in this a reflection of Strauss's increasing self-confidence, others merely saw inflation. For each writer such as Karl Schmalz, who saw *Zarathustra* as a decisive change for the better, even an attainment of mastery, there have been others such as Ernest Newman who predicted obscurity for it (at least in comparison with the earlier, conciser tone poems).[5] But the difference of opinion reflects one curious aspect of the work. In the process of acquiring the scale of the nineteenth-century symphony, it rejected many external traits of the symphony's form. As a result, its structure posed considerable difficulties for commentators (see chapter 7).

Part of the problem for *Zarathustra*'s critics was the programme. This, however, opened an area of controversy that seems to underlie virtually every facet of the work. The question of programme music is in fact a network of overlapping questions that embraces not merely its status in relation to absolute music, but also the problem of what is appropriate to a programme. Although both aspects will loom large in the following pages, it is the latter which undermined faith in *Zarathustra* among Straussians. Here the problem is not so much whether Strauss wrote a tone poem 'about' Nietzsche, as whether he should have done so. Thus Norman Del Mar doubted the wisdom of composing 'music about a visionary philosophy', and devising 'a piece of purely orchestral programme music around a series of ideological utterances' (assuming that these were Strauss's intentions).[6] He followed a distinguished line of Straussians, including Waltershausen, who held it 'self-evident ... that no living musical form can emerge from the speculative basis of the material', and the critic Leopold Schmidt, who took the opportunity to restate his initial doubts in a volume of essays to which Strauss himself provided the introduction.[7] The word 'frei' in the subtitle seems to have been designed to undermine, if not refute, such doubts. But it also looks suspiciously like an attempt to forestall more general objections to the writing of 'symphonic poetry' at a time when the debate about programme music was as sharp as at any time in the nineteenth century (see chapter 5).

Most critics of Strauss's time were fully aware that programme music had existed before Liszt's symphonic poems. Yet the question of the validity of programme music, or more specifically, illustration and narrative in music, was debated even more vigorously on the battleground of Strauss's tone poems than in the past. Arguably the debate was founded upon a misunderstanding. As Carl Dahlhaus has noted, under the prevailing influence of Schopenhauer, 'absolute music and program music, symphony and symphonic poem, were linked in a manner that flies in the face of popular aesthetic clichés about the "formalism" of the one and the "formlessness" of the other'. The basis of the link lay in the belief that programmes might initiate works as 'form motives' or present aids to interpretation (as they do in both Liszt and Strauss), but that they could not compensate for flawed structure by literary coherence;[8] this view stands behind Strauss's oft-quoted and apparently surprising insistence that 'so-called programme music has absolutely no existence'.

It is a term of abuse in the mouths of all those who can imagine nothing of their own. In the same way, the word kitsch is a favourite of those who, like the fox leering at the grapes, envy the 'effect' which the *Tannhäuser* or *Oberon* overtures or Schiller's *Räuber* make. . . A poetic programme can truly be a stimulus to new formal structures, but where the music does not arise logically from itself, it becomes 'literature music'.[9]

If this represents a Schopenhauerian view, then it is difficult to disentangle from Lisztian practice. Strauss had no doubt that the 'fundamental principle of Liszt's symphonic works, in which the poetic idea was also at the same time the element shaping the form', had become 'the guiding principle of my own symphonic work'.[10] This is certainly explicit enough and suggests that if Strauss distanced his tone poems from Liszt, he must have required strong support from factors other than the aesthetic. In context, however, it is important to remember that Strauss knew not only Liszt's symphonic poems and their defence in Liszt's prose works, but also Wagner's critique (see chapter 2).

In the last resort, Strauss wrote 'tone poems' only partly as a result of specific influences from Liszt and Schopenhauer. As Dahlhaus has pointed out, the use of 'poetic' in Liszt (but also in Schumann and many other nineteenth-century writers on music) was not an aesthetic or technical description but a value judgement that reflected a general trend; as poetry sought increasingly to be musical, so music sought to acquire the poetic, not by the prose of programmes but in its own right.[11] Thus Nietzsche compared his *Also sprach Zarathustra* to music (*EH* 295), it was frequently described as a prose-poem, and Strauss reworked it 'freely' as a tone poem; the categories of aesthetic description appear to break down. Later, the 'musicality' of Wilde's prose-play *Salomé* would be taken over by the apparently 'naturalistic' illustration of Strauss's music.

Nonetheless, it was one thing to write programme music under the aesthetic aegis of a philosopher (Schopenhauer), quite another to write music 'about' a philosopher (Nietzsche). In applying the title *Also sprach Zarathustra* to his tone poem, Strauss entered a sphere of ideas that did indeed seem to lie beyond music, but only as long as Nietzsche's philosophy was considered in its destructive mode. Among Strauss's contemporaries, there were in effect two perceptions of Nietzsche. On the one hand was the destroyer of nineteenth-century idols, chiefly religion. The agent of destruction was above all the aphorism, short, startling, and designed as the explosive prelude to a wider critique. In his critical books, Nietzsche directed his attack against the 'herd' morality of Christianity, elevating in its place a species of individualism that chimed with a certain strain of libertarian thought in Strauss's intellectual surroundings (see chapter 2). Eventually, the individual of Nietzsche's philosophy took on the infinitely richer shape of the Superman, who is identified at peril with the 'blond beast' of Aryan imaginings; rather he is to be seen as the revaluer of morality through the Will to Power, as the incarnation of the central Nietzschean idea of Eternal Recurrence. In the figure of the Superman, Nietzsche created the second side to his message, the positive of life-affirmation. In *Also sprach Zarathustra*, the figure of the Superman carried individualism forward into a picture of saying yes to life that sought to replace the values of religion and the herd. The Superman was equated with the acceptance not merely of life, but of death as the necessary condition for life, the tragic background that made the infinitely recurring circumstances of life a cause for celebration.

In practice, this double image was not always easy to perceive and interpret. Amongst the critics of Strauss (see chapter 5), the image of the destroying (and hence unmusical) Nietzsche was always to the fore, with this much justification: books such as *Also sprach Zarathustra* depended upon a startling juxtaposition of the aphoristic and the rhapsodical, which effectively placed the revaluation of values even at the heart of life-affirmation. More subversive was the implication in Nietzsche that an element of parody lay underneath even the positives of his philosophy. Among Strauss's admirers, the destructive Nietzsche took second place to the poetic and musical qualities of his language and images (while the parodistic qualities were ignored). The 'poetic' Nietzsche became an article of faith (and indeed has also haunted writing on Delius in an odd, distorting fashion). In Strauss's letters, there was a tendency at times to separate the poetic from the critical in Nietzsche, though Strauss was clearly at one period fascinated by both. As a consequence of this separation, Straussians have often taken 'freely after Nietzsche' as a reflection of the poetic strain in the philosopher, thereby refuting suggestions that Strauss had sought to set philosophy to music. The poetry was in the language, which some Straussians naively viewed as separable from the philosophy.

Strauss took Nietzsche's book as a hermeneutic aid by scattering a group of Nietzsche's section headings through the score. The exact status of these headings is a confusing factor in the literature about Strauss's work, though few writers have made the mistake of assuming that the musical sections represent a simple depiction of the corresponding parts in Nietzsche's book. Broadly speaking, the problem is the degree to which they acted as incentives to Strauss's musical imagination. In this, Strauss's own comments in his sketches offer little help, since they provide a rather more oblique picture of the way in which composition and programmatic factors interact. But the key word here is 'composition', the actual conceiving and writing-down of the work rather than the structure that analysis may discern in it. In the history of *Zarathustra*, three strands of literary allusion may be discerned, which parallel the processes of inception (chapter 4), elaboration (chapters 4 and 6), and reception (chapter 5); needless to say, the strands are not quite separate. But broadly speaking, Strauss chose to reveal the section headings, not to disclose the manner in which Nietzsche had guided his thought in composing, but as a means of illustrating the structural basis of the work in performance.

Reception, however, is never controllable by the composer. *Zarathustra* was destined to be received in more than one medium, as is evident from the moment that the completed work passed into the hands of the publisher's arrangers for transcription into a variety of combinations of hands and pianos. With the passage of time, it has acquired stranger contexts. Thus the present writer has performed in an arrangement for military band, in which the first section, according to some a scornful reference to revealed religion, became the emotional climax and final section; Nietzsche, as it were, for the Salvation Army. Then there was the version of the famous opening for Caribbean steel band overheard in a Liverpool community centre some time in the seventies. What was interesting here was not the extraordinary sound of the opening major-minor changing-chord emerging from a jangle of harmonics, but the comment of a neighbour, 'What would Strauss have said if he had heard his *2001* performed like this?' Kubrick's film created a mass audience for Strauss's music that has added another strand to reception.

As a result, perceptions of the work have changed in the last twenty-five years; from a dance of Dionysian life-affirmation, it has moved to something altogether more grandiose, as is reflected in the changing approaches to performance. Strauss's work of half an hour's duration has started to expand in recent performances and recordings, growing more monumental, perhaps even Wilhelmine (to anticipate a minor theme of Strauss reception). The history of the reception of *Zarathustra* thus is partly the story of the revenge of Nietzsche's 'herd'. A mass audience came to the work only as its original title lost its force at a time when Nietzsche's name tended to be viewed with some suspicion; it gave ground to a new central image which was created in the mass media of film and television. Whether this means that the work has conclusively revealed an 'absolute' basis beyond programmes is debatable; what is beyond question, however, is that programme and structure are not inextricably linked in describing and assessing the work, as Strauss would doubtless have recognized. If, in subsequent chapters, the sequence 'programme, then structure' is broadly followed, it is more as a musicological convention than as a statement about Strauss's indebtedness to Nietzsche.

2

The Straussian tone poem as drama

Strauss's career as a composer was already well launched when he aligned himself with the New German School (as the group around Liszt had been named). So pronounced had seemed his Brahmsian heritage that his conversion counted as a minor sensation. Steinitzer records this in his account of the critic Paul Marsop rushing up with the latest news, 'Strauss has now become a Lisztian!'[1] In practice, Strauss's commitment to a Lisztian point of view was always qualified. It is evident that he prized Liszt's capacity to convey a certain tone by harmonic means, without the need of conventional contrapuntal techniques. This quality could be regarded as poetic, but was by no means confined to symphonic poems. Strauss was thinking of the oratorio *Die Legende von der heiligen Elisabeth* when he observed that Liszt's sense of poetry was not dependent on counterpoint, but he could also have cited those places in Mass settings where composers traditionally reached for fugal techniques, but where Liszt in his 'Gran' Mass instead sought to create through harmony and orchestration a mood in keeping with the text. Strauss would have connected such moments to the linking of 'the triumph of harmony' and expressive potential in the writings of his favourite aesthetician, Friedrich von Hausegger.[2] Undoubtedly the idea of the poetic for Strauss was also dependent upon the nineteenth-century orchestra's greater range of tone-colour. This range Strauss sought to capture but not initially to expand. In *Macbeth* and *Don Juan*, the recognizably Straussian feature is the way in which the orchestra was used, rather than any novel colours (though *Macbeth* made telling use of the bass trumpet, and *Don Juan* of the glockenspiel). It is important to stress this factor from the outset, simply because the image of Strauss as illustrator or narrator would be unthinkable without his mastery of orchestral technique; the problems that critics found in his concept of programme music sprang in large measure from a purely musical ability to wield a purely musical instrument with remarkable vividness. Nonetheless, the Lisztian aspect of Strauss's musical heritage was more particularly expressed through his approach to symbolism, which in this context is less the use of specific tonal symbols than a central image.

The Lisztian symphonic poem and mythic symbols

The springs from which the symphonic poem flowed were many and varied, but Dahlhaus and Hans Heinrich Eggebrecht are undoubtedly correct in isolating the aesthetics of Kant and Herder.[3] Whereas Liszt subscribed in essence to Herder's view of art as myth and image, it was his object to remedy an apparent deficiency in Kant's aesthetic of music by providing it with concrete ideas. This was, however, a goal that required myth, image and symbol (Herder's stock-in-trade) to organize concrete ideas associatively. In Eggebrecht's terms, symbol and myth were to provide the 'conceptual thread of Ariadne' alongside a Kantian 'concept-free aesthetic'; together they would counter the tendency in the symphonic poem for traditional forms and genres to break down into 'configurations of diverging characteristics'.[4] Although Liszt made visible the cleft between formalism and the composer as poet, his characterization of the latter as composer of 'expression' never required music to surrender its own appropriate modes of discourse. Rather, his goal was quite compatible with musical means; symbol and myth were to resonate in sympathy with music, rather than to dictate to it. Characteristically, his central images select from a panoply of real and fictional heroic myths that would require little introduction to his ideal audience: Hamlet, Prometheus and Orpheus; Goethe, Shakespeare and Herder. For it is often the case that the creative figure (or the symbolic charge carried by his name) is the true hero of a Lisztian symphonic poem; in *Prometheus*, Herder's grand ideas are recalled at least as much as the Titan, for the simple reason that Herder based his drama on the moment at which Prometheus passed from suffering hero into a myth to be celebrated. Such a concept is even more apparent in *Tasso*. A consequence was that musical form tended to be determined by the image at least as much as by a literary argument. Admittedly, a work such as *Die Ideale* seems to contradict this by scattering lines from Schiller's poem through the score. But Liszt did not allow the lines to dictate, in so far as he changed their sequence in accordance with other factors that may have been personal or musical.

The parallel here with *Also sprach Zarathustra*, where the sequence of section headings departs from Nietzsche, is close enough to suggest that Strauss remembered Liszt's procedure; it is further strengthened when it is remembered that Schiller's poem aspires towards philosophical argument, while Nietzsche's book aspires to the state of poetry (and memorably achieves it in the song of the midnight bell). It is also not irrelevant that *Die Ideale* is one of the less easily classifiable symphonic poems where musical form is concerned. It has sometimes been suggested that the simpler forms employed by Liszt in *Hamlet, Prometheus* or *Orpheus* sprang from their status as overtures before they took their final form; a related idea is found in the suggestion that overtures were 'Ausdruck der Empfindung' ('expression of feeling'), while the symphonic poem was 'Malerei' ('painting'), in Beethoven's famous opposition.[5] The distinction is not invalid, but undoubtedly a work such as *Orpheus* suits its particular form because its guiding idea had little to do with visits to Hades or Orpheus's death at the hands of the Bacchantes; although *Orpheus* could stand on its own as absolute music (in a ternary form), its origins were in 'images of fantasy' which issued in musical symbols.[6] By comparison, works such as *Mazeppa* and *Hunnenschlacht* required more discursive forms because the central image was of a process rather than a mythical figure. In such contexts (and in *Tasso*), the feeling to be expressed involved that metamorphosis of struggle into triumph that the nineteenth century read in Beethoven's Fifth Symphony.

Strauss and the mythic in Nietzsche's *Zarathustra*

Such an approach is no less apparent in Strauss, whose comments on structure in programme music were governed by the idea that a central image should be 'associated with its sounding form as constituent factor'.[7] This is undoubtedly clearest in *Don Juan* and *Till Eulenspiegel*, where the differing characters of the central figures made the adoption of sonata form with episodes and rondo form admirably suited to a personal development and to a picaresque hero respectively. In both Liszt and Strauss, such conventions as the 'masculine' first subject and the 'feminine' subsidiary theme (a concept which in relation to 'absolute' music is of a banality that nowadays makes the critic blush) were precisely suited to such dual images as Hamlet and Ophelia, or Macbeth and his Lady; the additional episode in *Don Juan* arises as a consequence of the more protean sexual appetite of that hero, which required expression rather as King Duncan needed to be introduced into *Macbeth*.

With *Zarathustra*, an interesting situation arose in that the name carried a double resonance, thus reproducing a situation already familiar from Liszt. The central symbol had a double aspect reflecting historical personage and creative writer. In this case, the significance of the historical character was diluted to the point of merely evoking the image of a sage (rather as Mozart and Schikaneder employed an Italian form of Zarathustra for Sarastro, thereby endowing him with the aura of a religious leader and sage even before he begins to sing). Nietzsche was attracted to the name in the first place, one may assume, because of that aura, and built it into his Zarathustra to the point that it all but blotted out the original Persian model when Strauss came to write his tone poem. But that the name faintly carried that symbolic charge was overlooked often enough by those who thought the tone poem a reproduction of a philosophical argument or ideological tract.

The mythic element is still present in Strauss's *Zarathustra*, in spite of Nietzsche's own image as a destroyer of idols and myths. But there were additional strands to the myth. Nietzsche certainly studied the Persian background of the original Zarathustra.[8] From there (or possibly earlier), he arrived at an image of Zarathustra as life affirmer; the prophet first descends to mankind (or makes the bridge back from solitude to humanity) not at the start of *Also sprach Zarathustra* but at the end of Book 4 of *Die fröhliche Wissenschaft*, in the aphorism, 'Incipit tragoedia' ('The tragedy begins'). As the last title suggests, the journey to life-affirmation was to be far from a simple one, being a 'going under', a drowning in the tide of humanity in order to acquire the ability to live (*FW* 274–5). Later, in *Ecce Homo*, Nietzsche pointed out that the Persian Zarathustra, in his picture of the conflict of good and evil (personified in Ormuzd and Ahriman), had brought the 'most calamitous error, morality' into being; for him, it was essential that the originator of the error 'must also be the first to recognize it' (*EH* 327–8). Here lies the essential core of the figure of Zarathustra in Nietzsche's eyes. Zarathustra, having become myth, now acquires a hard tangibility that is aimed against myths and idols. In choosing this figure for a tone poem, Strauss proposed to remythologize the figure whom Nietzsche had so painstakingly rendered concrete.[9]

Ritter, Strauss, and the poetic

The reminiscences in which Strauss recorded his adoption of the Lisztian principle of symphonic poetry come (presumably) from late in his life. There is evidence, however, to suggest that they represent his earlier opinions with a reasonable degree of accuracy.[10] As early as *Macbeth*, on the other hand, there is no doubt that he was viewing the Lisztian tradition with a critical eye. 'Not after Liszt', that seemingly off-hand description of *Macbeth*, was written at a time when he was particularly close to his Lisztian mentor, Alexander Ritter

(1833–96), who had settled in Munich in 1885 after a career as violinist, conductor and music publisher in Weimar, Meiningen and Würzburg. The exact role of Ritter in shaping Strauss's taste is slightly obscured for us by the loss of their correspondence since Max Steinitzer had access to it in his pioneering study of Strauss. Its interest, presumably, would reside in large measure in the degree to which Ritter combined a poetic education in the principles of Liszt with an assessment of Wagner (whose niece Ritter had married). By the time of *Zarathustra*, Ritter's influence on Strauss had undeniably weakened (he died while Strauss was working on the score). Yet his impact for a time had been great enough to justify speaking of an intellectual circle dominated by him and embracing *inter alia* Strauss and his close friend Ludwig Thuille.[11]

In spite of the powerful influence of Ritter, Strauss still felt the need to distance himself from Liszt. In part, this may have been because of historical factors. The bulk of Liszt's symphonic poems lay thirty years in the past when Strauss started work on *Macbeth*, and they could not have been an entirely convincing model, given that the later operas of Wagner lay between. Ritter's doctrine (if it was ever so well-defined as that word implies) seems to have stressed the emptiness of the generation of Brahms and Bruckner (for whom Strauss, like Mahler, gradually came to have little sympathy). Where then was the link with the epoch of Liszt and Berlioz, where, in effect, was that New German School which Berlioz and Liszt were supposed to have initiated? For Strauss, such composers of programmatic music as Raff can have had little impact. Ritter himself had composed, and to writers with an eye for historical lines and traditions his music still seems worth investigating. So for Alan Walker,

A revival of [Ritter's] tone-poems, in particular, is long overdue, since they represent a bridge between Liszt and Richard Strauss. Incidentally, Strauss always maintained that it was Ritter who introduced him to the music of the New German School and helped him to break out of the conservative mould of his youth.[12]

The second sentence is certainly true, but it is surely legitimate to worry over the element of exaggeration in the first. For a start, Ritter avoided such terms as tone poem and symphonic poem, no doubt with very good reasons: the works that seem to conform by their titles to the Lisztian line of descent on inspection often seem conventional enough to recall the rather insipid picture of 'absolute music' to be found in Liszt's writings. Even Ritter's biographer, Siegmund von Hausegger, concedes that only one of Ritter's orchestral works, the 'Symphonische Trauermusik' *Kaiser Rudolfs Ritt zum Grabe*, resembles a symphonic poem.[13] It is, however, difficult to verify this statement, given that the work has never been published. Of those works which have, the 'Sturm- und Drangphantasie' *Sursum corda!* reveals a style still completely under the shadow of Liszt. The chromatic elements in his writing exhibit Liszt's fondness for augmented triads and diminished sevenths (rather than the Wagnerian half-diminished seventh). Themes are treated as characters, with a chorale on celestial strings used as an alternative to *Sturm und Drang*, before an apotheosis confirms the Lisztian impression already made by the use of thematic metamorphosis from introduction to the main Allegro. It is easy to share the doubts of Gerald Abraham about the musical validity of the relationship between Ritter and Strauss, and to relegate Ritter's influence to the not inconsiderable sphere of ideas (which is how Strauss himself tended to paint it, in spite of his services to Ritter's music in concert hall and opera house).[14]

Yet Abraham does note the anticipation of *Zarathustra* in *Olafs Hochzeitsreigen*, a work published the same year as *Zarathustra* (though it is several years earlier in composition). The link as described by Abraham is the tolling of a midnight bell towards the end of Ritter's work, though he does not go on to note that the two works are further linked by the waltz rhythms into which the bell strikes: the subtitle of *Olafs Hochzeitsreigen* is 'Symphonischer Walzer'. Ritter is not as ambitious as Strauss, specifying a tam-tam where Strauss wanted a real bell. Nonetheless the parallel is worth stressing, not least because 'Olaf' seems more consciously modern in its harmonic vocabulary than *Sursum corda!* There is less Lisztian thematic transformation as well, with the tritone acting as a fate leitmotif. The theme of the work is a wedding feast which terminates at midnight with the execution of the groom; this is Olaf's reward for a marriage which his king disapproved of, but could not prevent. The parallel with *Zarathustra* is thus mainly musical, though as such it is interesting enough, with the bell's interruption causing the waltz to split into fragments and ebb away in both cases. But to compare the two is to realize afresh the immense distance that separated the two composers. For Ritter's waltz, intended as the expression of rapture, is really a very conventional dance; by comparison, the waltz music in *Zarathustra* may be as vulgar as its critics imply, but it is a vulgarity of truly monstrous abandonment. Ritter's musical talent was simply not adequate to the role that Walker would like it to play.

As a consequence of the gulf that separated him from Liszt, Strauss was able to interpret the pre-history of the tone poem rather more freely than might have been apparent from Ritter's insistence on the Lisztian heritage. Strauss preferred to set himself in the tradition of Beethoven and Wagner. Part of this must inevitably be traced to the nineteenth century's obsession with Beethoven and his symphonies. As early as August 1888, Strauss wrote to Bülow of the need to link up 'with the Beethoven of *Coriolan*, *Egmont*, the *Leonore III* Overture, of *Les Adieux*, above all with late Beethoven, whose complete œuvre, in my opinion, could never have been created without a poetic subject'. In his view, this was the only possibility for the 'independent further development of our instrumental music'.[15] The need is related to his own sense of the incongruity of his kind of 'musical-poetic content' and classical sonata form. Such content was defined in terms of mood, structure and impression. The mood must be unified, the structure consistent, and the impression 'clear and definite'. The latter could only arise through a poetic idea, though Strauss did not regard a programme as absolutely essential to this. He concluded his outline of his new kind of instrumental music by stressing the need for new forms to arise for 'every new subject', and dismissed the possibility of 'purely formalistic, Hanslickian music-making'. Although this was the programme for a specifically new type of music, there is little that is new about the formulas employed. Strauss seems to hark back to the mid-nineteenth century in his stress on the poetic idea, the reverence for Beethoven, and the condemnation of formalism. What was different was merely the historical context: Strauss writes as though previous thinking on the same subject had not exhausted the possibilities.

The symphonic poem as character sketch; the tone poem as drama

Where Strauss placed Liszt in this line from Beethoven is made explicit in a long letter to Thuille over two years later (on 19 November 1890).[16] Here the *Faust-Symphonie* (1854) is singled out as the work whereby Liszt achieved 'a giant step forward' from Beethoven. Beginning with praise 'even' for its adoption of a multi-movement design, Strauss posited a difference between the third movement, 'Mephistopheles', as 'the real dramatic action', and the first two movements, 'Faust' and 'Gretchen', as 'symphonic poem'; the figures of the latter were 'so complicated that their *portrayal* together with the development of the action was quite impossible in a single movement'. By implication, 'symphonic poem' stands for character depiction without action or narrative. Just what kind of action Strauss envisaged in 'Mephistopheles' is not so clear, though he did note that the figure of the demon was introduced into the 'Faust' movement, and that the two different types of movement were equally imbued with 'poetic musical expression'.

Having thus linked Liszt to Beethoven, he then disposed of the connection with Berlioz by means of a further comparison with Beethoven. The discussion shifts to instrumentation. Opposing the idea that modern orchestral technique had originated with Berlioz before passing to Wagner, he stressed that Beethoven was the true originator because of his capacity for increasing 'the expressive potential of the individual instrument' (whereas he seems to see Berlioz, at this point, as more of a practitioner of 'expanded means'). Weber was the heir of this expressive instrumentation.

In all of Berlioz, no instrument speaks in such specifically human language as the clarinet in the *Freischütz* overture or the bassoon in the finale of the third act.

This seems palpably unfair on Berlioz, not least because Strauss turned against the Frenchman the very clarinet example which he had himself repeatedly and famously extolled. But Berlioz has good company in the dock. An entire generation of Romantic thought seems to be dismissed in Strauss's concluding words:

. . . the expanded orchestral apparatus of the 'Ring' is not the consequence of the longing for unknown, exquisite sounds in *themselves*, but of the drive for new expression.

To see this as a preference for realism over Romanticism is perhaps to read too much into one sentence of a letter. Nonetheless, Strauss's concept of the poetic idea had clearly taken a much harder shape than earlier aestheticians and composers would have recognized in their favourite terms.

The capacity of musical instruments to express seems to be an important factor in the new poetic music, whether in dramatic action or symphonic poetry. It is small wonder if writers have tended to see Wagner's impact on the writing of symphonic poems (and by extension of tone poems) in orchestral terms.[17] Yet the reference to drama in the context of instrumental music (which 'Mephistopheles' is, if the vocal conclusion is regarded as an epilogue to the whole work rather than to the third movement) may suggest other ways in which Wagner came to influence the development from symphonic poem to tone poem. At the very least, there was the influence of Wagner's theorizing, which left its mark on the sketches of *Zarathustra*. Virtually an entire side of Strauss's Sketchbook No. 2 is taken up with a little dissertation on musical drama in an instrumental context:

17

What is known as 'working-out' or 'development' is something that is in opposition to the possibility of the existence of today's 'absolute' music. Let the character tell us clearly what it is, then the hearer has something to latch on to, let its conflict with the other characters of the small, purely human drama be limited to the briefest intimations, which will be understood by the listener who really hears the music, even if his nose hasn't been rubbed in it seven times, while the layman can use them as a source of information until, within a short time, a new 'character' offers itself to him.

The excessive length of the development is something which Wagner rightly found to be a failing in the Lisztian symphonic poem.[18]

The reference to Wagner probably concerns Wagner's 'open letter' on Liszt's symphonic poems, which is fundamentally in sympathy with Liszt's aims, though its tone led to some degree of misapprehension as to Wagner's true intentions; thus Strauss stressed the negative dimension, while Dahlhaus underplayed it.[19] But Strauss's comments are not so much considered criticism as thinking aloud, an attempt to come to a clear picture of what instrumental music might be capable of attaining.

The idea that an instrumental work might be a 'drama' was expounded by Wagner in the Paris essay, 'De l'Ouverture' (1841), where *Leonore III* was described as 'a drama . . . in the most ideal meaning of the term'.[20] In 'Über die Anwendung der Musik auf das Drama', an essay published over forty years later, he returned to this subject in order to stress the 'circumspection' with which Beethoven had used the overture form as an 'occasion for the employment of purely musical means of expression in a form departing from the symphonic movement'.[21] The problem for Wagner was that development had led the listener to the denouement (represented by the trumpet signal), which was then delayed by the recapitulation. Much of this essay is devoted to distinguishing between the kinds of motives that are appropriate for symphonic and dramatic development respectively. Liszt actually plays quite a dignified role in the argument in contrast with the 'excesses' of a Berlioz.

This had already been amplified in Wagner's 'Über Franz Liszts Symphonische Dichtungen', which features the same cast of characters. Once again, Wagner doubted the value of maintaining the traditional form in *Leonore III*, and the excesses of Berlioz come into clearer focus. The 'Love Scene' in *Roméo et Juliette* fell short of the 'thoroughly compact *ideal* form' of a 'true musical poet' by too slavish an adherence to Shakespeare's dramatic process.[22] Once again it is arguable that Berlioz is being grossly misrepresented in the cause of expressing an ideal type; indeed it is arguable that Liszt is also being misrepresented, or at least severely limited, when cited as an exponent of the ideal type, for (as Dahlhaus notes), Wagner always refers to the more obviously ideal Lisztian works (such as *Prometheus* or *Orpheus*) at the expense of more discursive types.[23] But in spite of Wagner's praise of Liszt over Berlioz, his praise has an edge. Liszt often defined the ideal of the subject so well in the 'first sixteen bars' that Wagner felt moved to call out, 'Enough, I have it all!'[24] Liszt's symphonic poems hardly required their 'working-out', in other words, because the essential character was caught in a single musical idea.

This helps to define Strauss's aims. His concept of instrumental music was dramatic in the sense that it was to embrace ideal types or characters in conflict with others of the same kind. Lisztian development (including thematic transformation), already virtually indicated as unnecessary by Wagner, was to contract, a procedure which is immediately apparent in *Zarathustra*. That the remarks on the sketch were in some way a preparation for *Zarathustra* is suggested by the brief working-out of the Disgust motive (Ex. 3) which Strauss appended to his comments. In place of extended development sections in *Zarathustra* are parallel sections such as 'Von der Freuden- und Leidenschaften' and 'Das Grablied'; these verge on the self-contained but appear as two related but distinct types of experience, a metaphor suggested by their common material but different keys. The two extended fugal sections, 'Von der Wissenschaft' and part of 'Der Genesende', are developmental yet also characters, 'representing' certain types with old-fashioned abstract polyphony set against more modern 'developmental' counterpoint. Development is thus subject to the themes as embodiment of characteristics or even characters. The urge to compare these with the Wagnerian leitmotif reinforces the extent to which Strauss sought to synthesize into a single movement the character-sketch of the symphonic poem and the dramatic development which he discerned in 'Mephistopheles'. This synthesis of leitmotivic drama and character-sketch is the essence of the tone poem as opposed to the symphonic poem, and *Also sprach Zarathustra* is the most ambitious formulation of such a synthesis in Strauss's œuvre.

3

Strauss's individualism

It may be an elementary point, but it is worth remembering that Nietzsche was still alive when Strauss composed *Also sprach Zarathustra*. The impact of his philosophy was still fresh, *Also sprach Zarathustra* having appeared in its entirety as a single-volume, four-part work only in 1893. For much of the long composition history of *Guntram* (1887–93), Strauss could not have read the fourth part of *Also sprach Zarathustra* unless he had access to one of the private printings arranged by Nietzsche for his friends in 1885. Nietzsche's dramatic mental collapse took place in 1889, and by the time Strauss started to read him seriously, it was apparent to the philosopher's increasing body of admirers that his career was closed. Strauss thus found himself in the position of writing a work inspired by a philosopher who, though alive, could never discuss it with him. There is no guarantee that such a hypothetical meeting would have been fruitful, given the lack of meaningful contact in the parallel case of Wagner and Schopenhauer. Serious discussion would also certainly have broken down at the first mention of Wagner, on whom their positions were irreconcilable; Wagner remained one of Strauss's idols, whereas to Nietzsche he was one of the principal idols to be destroyed. This reflects a more general problem that Strauss found with Nietzsche's writings. However much he came to admire them, his professional awareness of the composition process and the history of music baulked at Nietzsche's alternatives to Wagner. In a letter to Cosima Wagner (10 April 1893), he noted that Nietzsche's 'longing for the south in music is comic in the extreme'; it is possible that an element of flattery enters into this, since Cosima was hardly the person to listen humbly to unadulterated praise of Nietzsche, but the sentiment rings true as a reflection of Strauss's attitude to Nietzsche's advocacy of a Mediterranean music against the composer of *Parsifal*.[1]

The musician remembers Nietzsche mostly for his advocacy and rejection of Wagner, for his espousal of Bizet's *Carmen* as the epitome of Mediterranean serenity, and for his wide-spread influence on a subsequent generation of composers. To others, he is the disseminator of the antithesis Apollo-Dionysos, interpreted as the clash of the rational and post-Socratic with the instinctive and irrational. In vulgar perception, he was for long regarded as a precursor of the Nazis, though this was largely forced upon his work by his sister, after he had sunk into his final years of insanity. More accurately, he came to embody an anti-Christian strain in nineteenth-century thought that attacked and 'overcame' (a favourite concept) conventional morality.

Also sprach Zarathustra was widely perceived as his masterpiece, the work in which he most clearly expounded a doctrine as opposed to shattering the systems of others. To explain it is far from straightforward, not least because of the underlying sense of parody that almost amounts to mischief. This is perhaps most clearly sensed in Zarathustra's claim to be a poet, while maintaining that 'all poets are liars' (in the section 'Vom Dichtern'). The paradox undermines any simple faith in what Nietzsche says through Zarathustra; but undoubtedly simple faith was the last thing that Nietzsche wanted. The central tenets of the book are 'the revaluation of all values', the Eternal Recurrence, the Will to Power, and the advent of the Superman, but in a sense these are all one and the same thing. The Superman was conceived not as a racial fantasy but as a realization of the potential for living in man. The revaluation of morality which he embodied was aimed against conventional religion and was expressed as the Will to Power, which is synonymous more with living life than with achieving political power. The Will in this context is neither the aimless and implacable prime cause found in Schopenhauer's philosophy (which Nietzsche aimed to revalue almost as a first essential step), nor the violent exercise of a collective mind embodied in the totalitarian state of the twentieth century; it is the property of the liberated individual. How the Eternal Recurrence comes to exemplify this Will is explained later in this chapter.

The book is part narrative, part collection of aphorisms (though these are not gathered together into discrete sections as in other works by Nietzsche), part discourses on topics. The topics in turn may deal with the conventional concerns of philosophy, or with the particular Nietzschean insights. The headings that Strauss took for his tone poem stand over sections in Nietzsche that blend narrative, aphorism and discourse into a unique literary genre (and Nietzsche was also one of the greatest German prose stylists). But these section headings do not give the whole picture of Strauss's fascination with Nietzsche and his book. Beyond them lies the broader question of intellectual kinship which involved Strauss in the history of ideas. It is complicated by the rather indolent, anti-intellectual outlook that is nowadays associated with Strauss, and which he took some trouble to maintain. But it would be a mistake to assume that Strauss's philistine exterior reflected an absence of interest in ideas. In the eighties and nineties this was clearly not the case.

Strauss and anarchist individualism

By his own account, Strauss had musical reservations about Nietzsche at a time when, according to some writers, he was coming round to espousing the Nietzschean philosophy. This leads directly into one of the principal controversies of Strauss biography. At its simplest, it is established that when Strauss began work on *Guntram*, he immersed himself in Schopenhauer on the encouragement of Ritter. Equally clearly, by the time the opera was finished, Strauss had moved on to read Nietzsche (who was anathema to someone like Ritter on account of his very public 'overcoming' of the influence of Wagner and Schopenhauer). The '*Guntram* chronicle' provided by Willi Schuh shows that Ritter had begun to worry about Strauss's interest in Nietzsche by February 1893, although Strauss assured him that he had never read *Jenseits von Gut und Böse* (the book by Nietzsche that immediately follows *Zarathustra*). There is no doubt that at this time Strauss was still digesting Schopenhauer's philosophy of the Will and of the need to renounce it, as a letter to Thuille shows (13 February 1893).[2] Yet the same letter indicates that Strauss had 'a few modest reservations', possibly about Schopenhauer's emphasis on the need to renounce the Will, that prime mover in human history which drove man on from one disaster to another.

The reason for the sense of crisis in the letters that mark the creation of the final act of *Guntram* lies in Strauss's decision to change his libretto, which had originally ended with a gesture of renunciation, but which was now altered to an assertion of the individual's right to control his own destiny. To Ritter, this was an artistic blot that seriously affected his relationship with Strauss. To make matters worse, Strauss soon began to read Nietzsche, and in particular *Jenseits von Gut und Böse*, the very book which he had denied reading to Ritter. Initially Nietzsche proved a source of confusion, which drove him back, as he told Cosima, to Schopenhauer. Yet *Jenseits von Gut und Böse* contained 'ideas which seem to me amongst the most significant that a human brain can invent', and its 'anti-democratic strain' was 'highly sympathetic'.[3] This (or another similar letter now lost) seemed to Strauss on reflection so potentially disastrous to his relationship with Ritter, that he begged his father (to whom he had sent it for forwarding) not to show it to him.[4] To grasp the full significance of Strauss's worries, it is important to realize that another of his closest friends, Friedrich Rösch, was opposed to Nietzsche's ideas though not to the extent of failing to attend the première of *Also sprach Zarathustra* in 1896.[5] The danger existed of a serious breach in Strauss's Munich circle. Yet this did not deflect him from his new, 'individualistic' ending for *Guntram*.

The main focus of the controversy, however, was not whether Strauss read Nietzsche at any stage while working on *Guntram* (the answer being clearly in the affirmative), but whether the new ending was prompted by this. The problem arose simply because Arthur Seidl wished to see the ending of *Guntram* as a decisive realignment of Strauss's intellectual position with Nietzsche (and others of a related strain), and expounded this view in a short biography which seemed to have the composer's blessing. Needless to say, it was then reproduced in other writings on Strauss, if not in the extreme form suggested by Seidl, who depicted Strauss as an 'ideal anarchist' warring against aesthetic and moral conformities.[6] If the controversy rested upon a variety of misapprehensions among Strauss's friends and fostered by his biographers, it cannot be denied that Strauss was soon studying Nietzsche closely enough to discuss him with Seidl in Weimar in 1893. In May 1894, he was already discussing another 'individualistic' writer with Seidl, John Henry Mackay, the author of *Die Anarchisten* and biographer of Max Stirner, a major figure in anarchist literature. Here was further fuel for Seidl's theory that Strauss was gradually 'overcoming' Schopenhauer and moving to a position associated with Nietzsche, Mackay and Stirner, in which the 'self-justification of the individual' was the key factor.[7] What Seidl was right to stress was the continuity of Strauss's thought from the conclusion of *Guntram*; but Strauss seems to have found confirmation of certain aspects of his own make-up in Nietzsche and the rest, not a complete reorientation. Whether Strauss approved of the particular interpretation that Seidl had projected on to him is not clear; however useful Seidl was to him, there is evidence that Strauss sometimes found his aesthetician's approach trying.[8]

On the face of it, Strauss does seem to have been remarkably open to libertarian, individualistic ideas throughout the decade of the nineties, and probably beyond to *Salome*. That opera indeed marks an epoch in its use of a play by the author of a libertarian tract on socialism (Oscar Wilde), translated into German by the wife (Hedwig Lachmann) of the anarchist poet, Gustav Landauer, who was eventually to die the death of a revolutionary. Ritter's worries about Stirner are often coupled with those about Nietzsche in the correspondence of the *Guntram* period.[9] But the project that seems to have been closest to Stirner's influence was the opera on Don Juan that Strauss considered in 1892. Much of the impetus for this came from Mackay whom Strauss had met in Berlin that year. In succumbing, however briefly, to the combined influence of Stirner and Mackay, Strauss moved into that peculiar area of the political spectrum where opposed extremes appear to meet. Although Stirner is one of the major figures of European anarchism, both he and Mackay have been attacked as middle-class ideologues and early proto-fascists.[10] Needless to say, such attacks are countered by equally vigorous defences. A somewhat different controversy is the precise degree to which Nietzsche 'followed' Stirner, which has been over-estimated by not a few writers; Mackay himself pointed out that a reappraisal of Stirner (to which the somewhat surprising figure of Hans von Bülow contributed) had been a consequence of the growth of interest in Nietzsche.[11] Nonetheless, Nietzsche, in respecting rather than aping Stirner, remained true to his own view of intellectual kinship.

Stirner's radical brand of individualism, in which the unique ego stood uncompromisingly opposed to the state to the point of denying society, was expounded in *Der Einzige und sein Eigentum*, a title usually translated as *The Ego and his Own*. The word 'Einzige', however, also conveys the idea of 'the unique' or 'the sole one', thereby defining rather more closely the main property of this 'ego'. It is in this area of unique individuality that Nietzsche, Stirner and Strauss come together. When Strauss expressed his distrust of democracy in the letter to Cosima of 10 April 1893, his position was by no means irreconcilable with Stirner's, since parliamentary democracy (particularly in a form so tethered by the state as in Wilhelmine Germany) was merely one of those institutions to which Stirner would have opposed the spontaneous uprising of unique egos. Mackay, however, diluted the potential violence of Stirner's message by rendering it compatible with private property, and so may have made it more acceptable to Strauss, who did not show a pronounced regard for *Der Einzige und sein Eigentum*. By the time Strauss composed *Also sprach Zarathustra*, the chief pointer to an individualist standpoint was the remark (almost a question) scrawled in Sketchbook 3 against the opening bars of the short score: 'Das Individuum tritt in die Welt oder die Welt ins Individuum' ('The individual enters the world or the world enters the individual').[12] There is no especially pronounced flavour of Stirner here, 'the unique one' having been replaced by the rather more Nietzschean 'Individuum'.

Nietzsche's concept of the individual

'Das Individuum' is the key to a central strand of Nietzsche's thought, and the term itself occurs fairly widely. It achieves prominence in works before *Zarathustra* (notably §132 of *Morgenröte* and §§57 and 618 of *Menschliches, Allzumenschliches*) and after it (as in §262 of *Jenseits von Gut und Böse*). There are inevitably examples of related terms such as 'Individuen' (as in §§143 and 149 of *Die fröhliche Wissenschaft*). But 'Individuum' is by no means the only term by which Nietzsche designates individuality, and 'Der Einzelne', or even 'Der Einsamste' ('the most lonely man', a label applied to Zarathustra at times) tend to be more common around the time of writing *Also sprach Zarathustra*. These alternative labels emphasize the solitariness and uniqueness of Nietzsche's concept of the individual. By the time of *Zur Genealogie der Moral* (which was an extension in 1887 of *Jenseits von Gut und Böse*), Nietzsche would have elevated the 'sovereign individual' to a central place in his philosophy, but the approach to *Zarathustra* reveals uncertainty as to the exact role of the individual; he goes so far in one text as to describe the individual as 'an error'. He seems at this point to have felt the need to overcome the individual ego in order to 'feel cosmically'. At least one writer has seen this struggle with overcoming the individual as a pre-condition for the emergence of the Eternal Recurrence, the central doctrine (apart from the Superman himself) of *Also sprach Zarathustra*.[13] But no less difficult for Nietzsche was the problem that individuality was both a hope and a curse, the latter in the sense that individuality was but a preparation for autonomy.

One must turn the curse of individuation into a feast. Without exception it is to be a tragic feast, but throughout the voice of creative freedom is nonetheless heard.[14]

The emphasis on creative freedom is significant, since the individual who finds his central role in 'violating pieties' (defined as such in §4 of *Die fröhliche Wissenschaft*) is also presented as a kind of artist-philosopher; this description flattered artists' egos in general much as Schopenhauer's picture of music emanating directly and guiltlessly from the Will boosted the self-esteem of a whole generation of musicians.[15] The extent of this creative role is most fully expanded in *Also sprach Zarathustra*, where the creator's act is that initially destructive 'revaluation of all values' associated with the Superman.[16] It is implicit throughout Nietzsche's thought that this creator-destroyer stands in opposition to the herd. This herd (which once possessed the faculty of creating) now has ceded its function to the individual, and submitted to conventional morality. Indeed it is the herd's fate to have created in the individual the agent of its own overcoming.[17] Since the ability to escape this herd morality of necessity involves its critique, the individual requires a critical gift that in turn extends to the reading of Nietzsche himself; the true Zarathustrian does not follow like a dog at the heels of its master but learns to live dangerously on his own account.

Whoever thought he had understood something of me, had made up something out of me after his own image – not uncommonly an antithesis to me (*EH*, 261).[18]

Nietzsche's individual then is not for all, indeed the degree of individuality is a measure of spiritual standing. Alongside this goes a variety of references to the herd that extend to a consideration of slavery; here is the dark side of Nietzsche's teaching with a vengeance. While the view that Nietzsche was a prime originator of fascism is clearly untenable, the more refined charge – the aesthetic similarity to fascism of his approach to the individual and the working class whose enslavement had made the modern individual possible – is a weighty one.[19] It is hardly surprising that Strauss found his 'anti-democratic' leanings reinforced by reading Nietzsche. Yet, as has been pointed out by Mark Warren, Nietzsche's attitude to the state was anti-totalitarian, favouring 'societies that sustain individual powers' over 'supraindividual institutions'. In this picture, the slavery of the herd is ambiguous, leaving doubt as to whether slavery is real economic subjugation or one of two potentials (along with self-certainty) for individuals.[20]

The relationship of the world to the individual is thus a central theme in Nietzsche, and profoundly undemocratic in its implications. As Strauss chose to express it in his sketches, however, this relationship is unclear. Strauss's comment on the individual's entering the world stands against music usually related to Zarathustra's going-down to humanity. But the reverse, the world's entry into the individual, is a more enigmatic concept, not unworthy to be expressed in the term World Riddle. This concept has been a staple of explicators of the tone poem (though it is not a central concept in Nietzsche) to the extent that it is a rival label to Nature for Ex. 1. Strauss elsewhere in the sketches equates this theme with the 'Universum'; this surely is an invitation to 'think cosmically'. Nietzsche's view of our perception of the world laid special stress on its ability to organize practical activity.[21] The central Nietzschean activity was that 'will to power' which in effect is identical to the 'revaluation of all values'; the philosopher paints a world in which values are related to individuation rather than linked to moral absolutes.

Values like those of Christianity that displace individuation are without value and hence nihilistic.[22]

But consciousness of the world is also linked rather directly at times by Nietzsche to man's social, rather than individual, nature, something that pertains to communication within the herd. The 'world entering the individual' of Strauss's marginalia is indeed a riddling concept in Nietzsche. What the world can tell the individual, according to 'Vor Sonnen-Aufgang' in Part III of *Zarathustra*, is 'deeper than anything the day has ever understood'. But Strauss set his World Riddle at, not before, sunrise: 'Die Sonne geht auf' precedes the remark about the world and the individual in the sketches. Sunrise therefore is not a guarantee of clarity in the Nietzschean scheme of things, and the riddle of Strauss's remark should accordingly be at its most enigmatic at the break of day.

The individual and the evolution of the Superman

Given such a world view, it is hardly surprising that the entry of the individual gives immediate rise to 'fromme Schauer' ('pious shivers'), as the short score designates the theme that enters in bar 23.[23] Clearly Strauss found comfort in Nietzschean individualism for his 'unconscious antipathy' towards Christianity's absolution of 'the believer (through the confessional) from personal responsibility and restraints'.[24] In Nietzsche's work, Zarathustra's first human encounter is with a pious hermit who does not know that 'God is dead'. Strauss may have taken this as a cue for introducing the whole tribe of the godly immediately after the start. But equally this may merely be rationalization after the event; in any critique of Nietzschean individualism, the 'revaluation' of Christian morality is an inevitable pendant. For Strauss, the shudder of the pious mind was simply opposed to the individual. It is possible that the critique of the religious mind was associated with the tone poem from the start, not as subject but as creative spark. Perhaps the most extraordinary clue as to the work's genesis was provided by Seidl when he claimed that its title was to be *Also sprach Zarathustra*, but that its 'subject' [*Gegenstand*] was *Menschliches, Allzumenschliches*.[25] As it stands, this remark seems absurd; if Nietzsche's *Zarathustra* was deemed unsuitable as a starting-point for instrumental music, how much more so was the earlier book, with its clinical aphoristic destruction of metaphysics and moralities. But *Menschliches, Allzumenschliches* does contain Nietzsche's first really direct assault on 'Das religiöse Leben'; perhaps therefore Seidl's remark contains this much truth, that Nietzsche's assault on Christianity was a major starting point, but hardly the subject, of the tone poem.

There is inevitably a large element of speculation in this, and it might well be objected that too much can be drawn from some remarks on a short score. Yet Strauss's description of the tone poem gives this interpretation some credibility. His stated intention, 'to convey in music an idea of the evolution of the human race from its origin, through the various phases of development, religious as well as scientific, up to Nietzsche's idea of the Superman', does capture that vision of the increase in individuality as growth in spirituality towards the Superman that is central to Nietzsche.[26] Strauss is not 'setting' *Also sprach Zarathustra*, but still wishes to convey something of its evolutionary outlook. But that was not his only description, and 'symphonic optimism in fin-de-siècle form' (as cited by several writers) makes a more general claim to that atmosphere of 'yea-saying' which is central to *Zarathustra*. Admittedly, Nietzsche's affirmation takes place specifically against a tragic background (an idea that is captured imaginatively in the dream of Hans Castorp in Thomas Mann's *Zauberberg*). But Strauss's qualification about 'fin-de-siècle form' is enough to bar this optimism from being a mindless celebration of good feeling. For some writers, this affirmation inevitably prompted memories of Dionysos, that central personification of the instinctive and irrational in *Die Geburt der Tragödie* who reappears, unnamed but unmistakable in the section of Nietzsche's *Zarathustra* entitled 'Von der grossen Sehnsucht'.[27] But such responses are inevitably metaphorical, the response of critics to the compelling musical images that Strauss created. At bottom, to think of Dionysos in listening to *Also sprach Zarathustra* has no greater validity than when Wagner invoked him while contemplating the Seventh Symphony of Beethoven.[28]

The Eternal Recurrence as affirmation of life

Equally, the notion of the 'eternal recurrence of all things', the most fundamental positive of Nietzsche's book, is something which at least one commentator has seen in the close of the work, as the B major conclusion is disturbed by C in the deep bass register with which the tone poem began.[29] The idea of recurrence is first made apparent by Nietzsche in the section, 'Vom Gesicht und Rätsel' ('Of the Vision and the Riddle'), when a dwarf (personifying Zarathustra's devil, the Spirit of Gravity) presents a riddle of a gateway marked 'Moment', from which two roads run infinitely into past and future. As described by Zarathustra, this is the riddle of the 'most solitary man' (not of the world). 'All truth is crooked,' claims the dwarf. 'Time itself is a circle.' This is the point at which Zarathustra, first angrily, then more softly as he becomes aware of the implications, expands this claim into a realization that all things which can happen in an eternity have happened in an infinite past and will happen again in an infinite future; all things eternally recur. The appalling nature of this discovery prompts Zarathustra into a vision of disgust at mankind which is later acted out by himself in 'Der Genesende', a title which Strauss took for perhaps the most involved section of his tone poem.

That the acceptance of Eternal Recurrence is the greatest form of 'yea-saying' gradually comes to dominate the later stages of Part III and is acted out as tableau in Part IV. Although Zarathustra for the moment proceeds on his way pondering the meaning of his vision, the real riddle is in the image of the roads and the gate, presented as a joke by the Spirit of Gravity, expanded gravely by the apostle of light feet and dancing, Zarathustra. In this insistence on time's circularity resides the beginning of Zarathustra's love of eternity, but once again it is in its way a tragic realization. As his animals interpret it in 'Der Genesende':

'Now I die and decay,' you would say, 'and in an instant I shall be nothingness. Souls are as mortal as bodies.

'But the complex of causes in which I am entangled will recur – it will create me again!'

If the opening of the tone poem truly is a World Riddle, then here is the greatest stumbling block to the individual's understanding of the world, but also its greatest affirmation.

If the 'fin-de-siècle form' of Strauss's optimism is to be understood as Nietzschean, then the tragic aspect of the Eternal Recurrence is its essential background. But nothing that Strauss wrote in letters, sketches and programmes actually spelled out a coherent system of thought dependent upon Nietzsche. He rather rested in the sphere of riddles and enigmas, content perhaps to offer his reaction to Nietzsche, which was consistent with that view of the critical individual expressed in *Ecce Homo*; there is nothing to contradict the view that neither Strauss nor Mahler (in his contemporary Third Symphony) 'tried to dissolve and convert Nietzsche's ideas directly into music, but rather . . . were inspired by them to produce basic ideas of their own work'.[30] On publication of his tone poem, Strauss allowed the group of titles to go forward for the sections, and these naturally encouraged, and still encourage, speculation as to his possible aim. To help control this speculation, he also approved the use of a programme book by Arthur Hahn to convey a series of hints as to content (such as the World Riddle) that was neither an outright expression of a Nietzschean point of view nor a rejection of Nietzsche's relevance. Throughout, he may have understated the extent to which he was in thrall to ideas, but this was in the interests of encouraging a more general and wide-embracing approach to the music, as 'free' an approach as he had adopted in composing the work. The section headings are only partly a description of a possible framework of ideas; they are also poeticized descriptions of musical content: religious chant, learned fugal style, modern contrapuntal style, dance and song. This point was sometimes obscured, not merely in the writings of critics but even in the insistence with which Strauss repeatedly characterized himself as 'expression' (in honour of Friedrich von Hausegger's *Die Musik als Ausdruck*). But Nietzsche's role as prompter of a musical drama does not imply that it is his drama which is recounted in the programme books.

The reception history of *Also sprach Zarathustra* can be retold as a battle between 'absolute' and programmatic points of view, but the 'absolute' label was claimed by friends and enemies alike. This is a measure of the extent to which Strauss absorbed his Nietzschean leanings into his mature musical inclinations. If *Also sprach Zarathustra* is a new direction or a climax in Strauss's output, it is because Nietzsche's promptings were in accordance with his desire to synthesize the symphonic poem and the instrumental drama into a shape for which an aphoristic manner was appropriate. If Strauss's aphorisms seem expansive by comparison with those of the Second Viennese School in the following decades, then this also reflects the fact that Nietzsche's style in *Zarathustra* lay poised between aphoristic truth and dithyrambic expression.

4

Composition and first performances

If the intellectual background of *Also sprach Zarathustra* remains complex, its composition history is relatively straightforward. The dates traditionally accepted for its composition are those supplied by Steinitzer, 4 February to 24 August 1896.[1] A copy of the full score in Strauss's hand survives today in Garmisch. According to Schuh, the first page is inscribed, 'Begun 4 February 1896, my beloved Paula's birthday', while Franz Trenner (Strauss's most recent cataloguer) gives the inscription 'Begun on 4 February, completed on 24 August 1896, Munich'. Neither writer (nor Mueller von Asow) is entirely clear whether this is a fair copy or Strauss's original working score.[2] The first sketches are described by Schuh as dating from February 1894, though by 9 July 1895 Strauss was still only at the stage of 'Thoughts about a new tone poem', which are listed in six categories. It is revealing of Strauss's approach to the work that these should be emotional states with no apparent reference to Nietzsche. In such words as 'contemplation' and 'worship' can be seen references to the 'scientific' and religious sections of the tone poem, but only with benefit of hindsight. 'Doubting' and 'despair' similarly are not without resonance in the light of 'Das Grablied' and 'Der Genesende', but 'experience' and 'recognition' are so vague as to convey little sense of a programme or musical content. Schuh describes them as 'key words in the conception', but they reflect a broad feeling for mood rather than specifics. Nietzsche seems to remain at arm's length in this draft, leaving the precise nature of the initiating spark shrouded in a mild degree of mystery.[3]

Strauss spent much of July 1895 in Cortina d'Ampezzo, from where he told Max von Schillings that he was doing nothing while letting 'great works "ripen within"'.[4] That his existence in Cortina was far from mere vegetation, however, is borne out by some work on *Lila*, his projected opera after Goethe. Less than a month later, Schillings expressed the hope that the ripening composition was the one 'with the two great *Melodie-Kränzen* in A flat major and C minor'.[5] This seems clearly to refer to *Zarathustra*, and the two melodic paragraphs concerned are almost certainly the sections later described as 'Von

31

den Hinterweltlern' and 'Von den Freuden- und Leidenschaften'. Neither theme appears in its entirety in Sketchbook 2, one of two sketchbooks in Garmisch containing material for *Zarathustra*, but there is a reference at one point to 'Passion theme in A flat major (brass, dark blue)'.[6] The surrounding sketches are for 'Das Tanzlied', suggesting strongly that this reference is to the transformed version of the 'Freuden- und Leidenschaften' theme which enters at bar 629; this waltz-time version of the theme duly appears a few pages later in the sketches. The two melodic paragraphs were thus part of an early stage of composition; it may even be possible to postulate a close chronological connection between the references in Strauss's diary to 'contemplation' and 'worship' and the A flat major melody of 'Von den Hinterweltlern'. In what form Schillings knew these melodies is intriguing. Schuh ascribes the beginning of 'planned systematic composition' to 7 December 1895, so it is possible that the ideas described by Schillings had merely been melodies without reference to a specific idea.[7] Whether they had actually been written down, or perhaps played by Strauss to Schillings in Munich, is unclear.

The labour of composition was largely confined to March and April of 1896 according to Schuh, who selected these dates as reflecting the key phase: 31 March to 4 April, 7 April to 11 April, and 13 April to 18 April. 12 April was the date of Ritter's death, an event which with cruel irony briefly halted the composition of a work whose title could only have caused him profound misgivings in the light of his strident objections to the *Guntram* ending.[8] On 12 April Strauss wrote to Cosima Wagner informing her of Ritter's death; in her reply of 13 April, she noted that it had touched her 'that your answer to the letter in which I wished you luck for your handsome behaviour on Ritter's behalf should now coincide with his death!'[9] This epistolary exchange also gave Strauss the chance to inform Cosima officially of his work on 'a symphonic poem which really will be called *Also sprach Zarathustra*'. The situation verges on the comical; Cosima obviously knew about the work, and Strauss equally clearly knew that she knew. Her reply was a masterpiece of condescension:

I had thought the title of your symphonic poem *So sprach Zarathustra* a newspaper's joke. But I don't know Nietzsche's book and now assume that there must have been something in it which inspired you to music.

So little did she know of Nietzsche's book, that she even got the title wrong. Indeed it is doubtful if the Bayreuth circle had read anything of Nietzsche's since *Menschliches, Allzumenschliches* was quietly put down after a few pages by Wagner himself.

On 24 June, Schillings received a more positive proof of *Zarathustra*'s progress in the form of a postcard with the notes c^1–g^1–c^2. By this point, however, one must assume that Strauss had progressed beyond the stage of sketching to the short score which is contained in its entirety in Sketchbook 3, together with its concluding date of 'Ende 17. Juli 1896'.[10] Strauss seems to have regarded the conclusion of this short score as the end of serious composition, since he wrote a few days later to Eugen Spitzweg, the proprietor of the publishing house of Aibl, that the work was finished.[11] By 7 September, he was also able to inform Schillings that the 108-page long full score of *Zarathustra* had been completed near the end of August. Since the weather in Strauss's summer retreat of Marquartstein had been bad, he provided Schillings with a teasing enclosure, the closing bars of *Zarathustra* in two-stave score, with the dialogue between high woodwind and basses turned into

Wann? nie! wann? nie! wann? nie! nie! nie! wird's schönes Wetter!

(When? Never! When? Never! There never will be fair weather!)

Even reduced to a weather forecast, the World Riddle naturally intrigued Schillings, whose curiosity can be seen as but the start of the commotion about the ending which long outlasted the first performance.[12]

The extant sketches for *Zarathustra* in Sketchbook 2 fall into several categories including real sketches of ideas and continuity drafts. The least tangible are those cases where Strauss sketched not musical ideas but a train of thoughts, the most extended of which is the meditation upon musical 'characters' and Liszt's development sections. Unfortunately, Willi Schuh's account of the annotations gives rather a false impression at times of Strauss's use of such marginal comments. Thus the whole of the following is described as being beside 'the theme C, E, G' (which is clearly a misprint for 'C, G, C'):

Remains immobile, rigid, unchanged to the end. Worship – Doubting / Doubt / Recognition – Despair – / reviving again in the red light of dawn / then 'Freedom' has made it its own. The priests are on the increase. Large diminuendo and extinction up to the beginning of the fugue, large build-up until all the Life themes come together! Their combination ends with Despair D minor, out of which finally Yearning B minor gently spreads its wings out over the one exhausted by the struggle with the ghosts of 'Life'. Leads B major and him to 'Freedom'. C major 3/4.[13]

These do not all belong together, however, being a collation of numerous comments occurring on different sheets. Some words refer back to the thoughts which Strauss noted down in Cortina ('Worship – Doubting / Doubt /

Recognition – Despair'), and here their context seems to be clear. They are part of a longer annotation accompanying a continuity draft beginning in bar 30. The horn theme that follows is marked 'credo in unum deum' as it was also to be in the published full score, but the following section for divided strings is represented only by the first two bars then 'As dur' and 'etc.' The whole of this section is thus treated as already composed (as is the C minor section, 'Von den Freuden- und Leidenschaften', in another continuity draft), and the sketch picks up the musical thread at bar 75. In addition to some indications of instrumentation, the marking, 'Sehnsucht' ('longing') is present. Subsequent events include the statement of 'c^1–g^1–c^2' in bar 82, marked 'engl. Horn', and 'Magnificat', referring to the organ. Below this Strauss wrote some of the comments translated above:

Thema c g c (Universum) immer unbeweglich, starr, unverändert/ bis zum Schluss. (Anbeten – Zweifeln / Zweifel / erkennen – verzweifeln – / wiederaufleben in / der Morgenröthe / Die 'Freiheit' hat sich's dann zu eigen gemacht[.][14]

This passage then refers to 'Von der grossen Sehnsucht', whose musical character indeed shows alarming fluctuations of pace, texture and emotion, before its sudden flare-up into the next section. The 'light of dawn' would seem to be the beginning of the next section, 'Von den Freuden- und Leidenschaften'; neither of the sections with these titles in Nietzsche's book make any reference to the 'light of dawn', however, and Strauss seems to be following his own chain of thought.

It is not the only reference to 'Morgenröthe' in the sketches. Trenner gives one comment as:

Kolossal steigern zum Schluss Morgenröthe Esdur erstes Sonnenthema / Schluss III. Akt

(Huge crescendo to the close Dawn E flat first sun theme / End Act III)

This stands below a very primitive (possibly the earliest) sketch for the 'Tanzlied', but the music below is almost certainly for *Lila*, and it is this to which 'Schluss III. Akt' refers. This leaves a slight puzzle as to where Dawn, E flat and the 'first sun theme' apply. Almost certainly they refer to *Zarathustra*, but they suggest a slightly different conception of the work at this point. Dawns and sunrises are a recurring theme in Nietzsche's *Zarathustra* (*Morgenröte* is of course the title of an earlier work by Nietzsche), and it looks as though Strauss had seized on this aspect; perhaps the 'first sun theme' is the theme of the universe, since it figures in the brief snippet of the 'Tanzlied', as in bar 409.

On the adjoining page to the continuity draft for 'Von der grossen

Sehnsucht', Strauss carried on in the direction of 'Von den Freuden- und Leidenschaften', but with surprises in the form of the Disgust theme which he ultimately reserved until bar 150, where it has a suitably prominent position in the trombones. Against it in the continuity draft, Strauss wrote 'Zweifel!' ('doubt' or perhaps 'suspicion'). The comment, 'Die Pfaffen nehmen / Überhand' (which might be better translated as 'The Priests prevail'), stands below a combination of Disgust, 'Credo' and 'Magnificat' which Strauss excluded from the finished work (it would belong at bar 98; here Strauss replaced them with the idea characterized on another page as 'Lebenstrieb', the 'life urge').

Some of Strauss's marginal comments thus refer to passages that are omitted because they were already drafted, others provide a commentary on Strauss's thinking as he composed. At other times they are simply labels. This is frequently the case when Strauss is working not with continuity drafts but with the sketching of basic ideas. Thus the first idea for the 'Tanzlied', on the same page as the music for the close of Act III of *Lila*, is labelled 'Tanzhymnus', a description that also occurs in the short score at almost the equivalent point (bar 409). The 'Lebenstrieb' idea is of two bars only, and under it another idea is drafted with the label 'niedrige Leidenschaften' ('lower passions'); this theme appears on one other page, but was not used in the composition; its key of E minor seems completely at odds with the finished work, where E has a negligible structural role. So to some extent does the D minor of 'Despair', which seems to relate to the fugue of 'Von der Wissenschaft' or to 'Der Genesende'. Some debatable traces of D may be seen in the latter, but again there is relatively little D in the work. Throughout there is plenty of evidence of the central role that C and B were to play, including a pair of chromatic progressions leading from a dominant seventh of C to B minor in the second inversion, and from a dominant seventh of D flat to C major in the second inversion; there is no better illustration of the way in which Strauss used the six-four as an agent of his more unexpected modulations. These particular progressions seem like plans for getting to the two main keys, though they correspond to no moment in the completed work. Perhaps the most surprising sketch is one for the final stages, in which the bell strikes C rather than E, and Strauss proposes 'dann ins Edur ganz für zuletzt' ('then into E major completely for the end'). Here again E has a role that ultimately was to vanish.

The marginal comments in the sketches therefore have three functions – as preparation for sketches, as descriptions of sketches and moments in the continuity drafts, or as substitutes for musical material in the continuity drafts.

In the short score, on the other hand, they are almost always descriptive. The short score is inevitably much more continuous, and there are by this stage few signs of uncertainty or revision in Strauss's mind. Of some twenty sides in length, it is mostly written in two- and three-line stave. Both score and margins are heavily encrusted with indications for orchestration which quite outweigh the descriptive comments. As has been suggested in the discussion of 'Tanzhymnus', these comments have elements of continuity with the sketches, but their greatest interest is when taken in conjunction with the programmatic hints outlined in Arthur Hahn's thematic guide (see chapter 6).

A problem arises from Schuh's dates, however, concerning the exact sequence of work on sketch, short score and full score. The probability is that whole sections, those most self-contained (such as the C minor and A flat major melodies), were in existence from a very early stage (possibly mid-1895), and that Strauss worked on short score and full score simultaneously rather than consecutively from February 1896. The difficulty of determining what Strauss was doing in the 'most intensive periods of work' is ostensibly further confused by a letter from Nikisch to Strauss of 3 February 1896. The publisher Aibl had already shown enough of the work in proof form to Arthur Nikisch by this date to convince him that 'it is a highly significant work of genius, and I am extraordinarily pleased to conduct it'; this seems utterly fantastic, however, and it is almost impossible to avoid the conclusion that this letter is badly misdated, as is confirmed by a further reference in the letter to the possibility of performing the work on 30 February [sic]; the letter should probably be dated 3 October, while the projected performance date must be 30 November, the day on which Nikisch did conduct the work in Berlin.[15] But even if this letter is grossly misleading, it is tempting to conclude that Strauss began work on his full score on 4 February while the short score was still incomplete. What remained to be worked out, given the existence of sections such as 'Von den Hinterweltlern', were open-ended sections and developmental links, which is consistent with that small dissertation on development sections in the sketches. The simultaneous work on both scores is consistent also with the short period of time between the completion of the particell (17 July 1896) and of the full score (24 August).

However doubtful the dating of Nikisch's letter, it remains of value as an indicator of the speed with which conductors responded to Strauss's works. The first performance of *Zarathustra* was to be given in Frankfurt am Main in the Saalbau on 27 November 1896, in the fourth Museum Society Concert of that season. The care which Strauss took over the first performances, however, is more fully documented for the concert of 1 December in Cologne.

This was the work's third outing after the premiere and Nikisch's performance in Berlin, and (as in Frankfurt), the conductor was to be Strauss. Franz Wüllner, the resident conductor of the Gürzenich Orchestra, had to take charge of rehearsals and other arrangements. As a result, there was some correspondence with Strauss over various details. Wüllner was planning as early as 4 June for a performance when the short score, let alone the full score, was not yet complete.[16] His preferred date was as early as 17 November, but this must have soon come to appear impractical. By 21 August, he was reduced to wondering whether the parts would actually be ready by 30 November, and asked if the piece was about as long as *Tod und Verklärung*. Later Nikisch would be told that parts would not be ready before 15 November.[17] For the moment, Wüllner had to rest content with the information on 24 August that '*Zarathustra* is very long and lasts nearly half an hour!'[18] By 22 October, he was insisting that parts had to be in Cologne by 20 November, and on 27 October Strauss had to write to Spitzweg with this information.[19] The problem was clearly solved to everyone's satisfaction, since orchestral material now disappears from Wüllner's correspondence with Strauss.

The next issue (in a letter of 24 November) was how much to tell the audience. The full score was prefixed by the opening address of Zarathustra, which is usually referred to in the Strauss literature as 'Zarathustras Vorrede', though this is actually the title of the whole first section of Nietzsche's book, embracing his going-down and first encounters with humanity. This address was not included in the Frankfurt programme, nor were the section headings from Nietzsche. For the Cologne performance, Wüllner favoured providing the titles but not the preface, but Strauss insisted on excluding both. His reasons were practical rather than ideological, however, since he hoped that Arthur Hahn's *Thematischer Leitfaden* would be on sale for the concert, and this included references to the titles. Whether it was on sale on 1 December is open to doubt, since the original pamphlet is usually described in catalogues as published in 1897 (though it carries no date); as a result, the audience were given access to the section headings in the programme book. Nonetheless the intention was clear. A greater worry for Strauss, however, was the order and contents of the concert. In the same letter, he hastened to inform Wüllner that the duration was in excess of half an hour, and urged him to cut the Schumann Piano Concerto and a choral piece from the programme, on the grounds that '*Zarathustra* makes demands on the public, which are quite impossible to meet after so much music.'[20] In this he was only partly to have his way, since Wüllner kept the Schumann (doubtless as a sweetener for traditionalists) but dropped the choral piece.

Before any of these performances took place, other conductors and venues were approaching Strauss for the work. Ernst von Schuch in Dresden was one possibility, though the connection between Strauss and Schuch was not then as firm as it subsequently became; it also seemed logical for Nikisch, having performed it in Berlin, to introduce it to Leipzig audiences.[21] One place where it had decided difficulties, however, was Munich. With his superiors in that city, Ernst von Possart (intendant of the court theatre) and Carl von Perfall (intendant of the court opera), Strauss was gradually falling out of sympathy, a process that led to his departure from the city in 1898. The dispute continued to rankle, and showed no sign of abating by the end of the century. Perfall turned down an offer from Strauss to conduct the work on 17 March 1899, which was probably an act of retaliation for Strauss's refusal to grant rights for a performance in a Munich Academy Concert in 1897.[22] In spite of this, *Zarathustra* went ahead, with the March performance under the baton of Fritz Fischer; Strauss himself did not conduct it in Munich until 16 March 1900. But Strauss did on one occasion take part in a keyboard performance of the work in Munich during this period, the other performers being Schillings, Thuille and Hugo Röhr. This presumably was in the transcription by Heinrich von Bocklet for eight hands at two pianos; there was also another performance by Schillings and Röhr in the Bayerischer Hof, and this was probably in the version for two pianos rather than that for one piano (four hands); both arrangements were by Otto Singer.[23] In such a curious fashion (which seemed in retrospect grotesque to Schillings) did Strauss introduce his new tone poem to his native city.

5

Reception

Programme music and its antagonists

The success of *Also sprach Zarathustra* in the concert hall was largely bound up with Strauss's conducting career. Although other conductors took it up, Strauss himself performed it on tours in numerous European cities. His letters document these as a succession of triumphs. In addition to his engagements in such German cities as Düsseldorf and Strassburg (as it was then), Strauss took *Zarathustra* to Belgium (Liège and Brussels), Amsterdam, Paris and Zurich before the century ended. As an indication of the acclaim with which *Zarathustra* was greeted, the first performance in Cologne may again be cited, with the work being accorded even more calls from the audience than the soloists received.[1] He took particular care to make sure that Spitzweg knew of the good impression that his latest publication was making.[2] Performances in Berlin seem to have been of a particularly high standard, and he considered one occasion in October 1898 as 'the finest performance of *Zarathustra* which I have experienced'.[3] His friends took these accounts of triumph at face value, though whether they accepted Strauss's valuation of the work as 'by far the most important of all my pieces, the most perfect in form, the richest in content and the most individual in character' is difficult to ascertain; that it was 'faultlessly scored' must have seemed all too credible.[4]

It went without saying, however, that a large critical faction found *Zarathustra* hard to take, and this did in time have its effect on performance and audience reactions. The Viennese press, in particular, had always taken a rather guarded attitude to Strauss (who claimed that his Violin Concerto had been the only piece that Hanslick had ever praised).[5] When *Zarathustra* reached Vienna on 21 March 1897, Hanslick's reaction was typical.[6] Over his review stood the words of Life to Zarathustra in 'Das andere Tanzlied' (words which form an indirect commentary on a rather more celebrated aphorism spoken to, not by, Zarathustra):

'O Zarathustra! Do not crack your whip so terribly! You surely know: noise kills thought!'

The tone was thus set from the outset. The other works in the programme, Weber's *Euryanthe* overture and the Fifth Symphony of Beethoven, were classed with mock innocence as 'two quite unphilosophically naive tone poems', before Hanslick turned to Strauss. Some play with the title (which should have been called 'a symphony for everyone and for no one' after the subtitle of Nietzsche's book) was then followed by consideration of the 'unmusical material'. In comparison, Liszt's sins paled into insignificance, since there was an understandable element in such titles as *Orpheus* and *Tasso*. Since Strauss had taken up with philosophers, it was an easy step to compare Richard I's Schopenhauerian extravagances with Richard II's 'step further' to Nietzsche. Inevitably Hanslick worried that the public would not be sufficiently acquainted with Nietzsche's difficult work, and noted that 'Zoroaster' and 'Sarastro' were better known and more likely to be recognized. The charge against Strauss is clearly one of mystification, bolstered with a venomous reference to Nietzsche's insanity that was worthy of Bayreuth. From here Hanslick plunged into a display of pseudo-scholarship about the *Zend-Avesta*, coupled with a gross travesty of Nietzschean thought as 'cynicism'. Nietzsche and Ibsen he regarded as the leaders of 'a type of philosophical Salvation or Calamitous Army ['Heilsarmee oder Unheilsarmee']'. Just as Nietzsche attempted to say in ten sentences what others expressed in a book, so Strauss attempted to say in ten bars what others said in a symphony; at the same time he complained about *Zarathustra*'s unprecedented length among symphonic poems.

Hanslick next turned his attention to the titles of the various sections of the work, and to a brief survey of its course, blending appraisal of individual moments with ideas culled from the programme (which suggests that he had been reading Hahn's explanations). Although he noted the poverty of the waltz, he rested content with citing a critic from Maximilian Harden's periodical *Die Zukunft* on the notorious ending. The inevitable charge was raised that the listener who was not forearmed with 'the detailed programme' would 'certainly not discover any connection with Nietzsche' in the work; *Zarathustra* was thus twice damned, for being programme music, and for not being explicitly programmatic; had it been explicit, then the charge of being merely illustrative lay to hand. The programme thus could be dismissed as an attempt to make the music seem more important than it was. Strauss's invention was 'uncommonly weak and tormented', and was sustained only by his ability with the orchestra, particularly in the arts of combining themes and producing adventurous timbral effects. This was the elevation of means into ends with a vengeance, and Hanslick backed up his objections by reference to the size of Strauss's orchestra.

From there it was back to Nietzsche, and speculation over further titles by the philosopher which Strauss might use. The moral dangers of the philosophy were equated with the perils of Strauss's music, especially for young composers who would be seduced from the paths of Brahms and Dvořák. Hanslick ended by acknowledging the efforts of Hans Richter at the head of the Philharmonic and the enormous applause, but consoled himself with the thought that this was probably more for the performers than the piece; for Beethoven's Fifth Symphony ('which did not once require trombones to make its mighty effects')[7] was even more enthusiastically received, leaving Hanslick to reflect that 'Strength and beauty of ideas are still more powerful than the most expensive apparel, and the true poet triumphs in the end over the most daring artifices of the stage-manager and the scene-painter'.

As on other occasions, the reader is left wondering at the contrast between Hanslick's scrupulousness as an aesthetician and the transparent intellectual dishonesty of his journalistic praxis. The review appears to write itself by means of a succession of clichés common to virtually every witty but conservative critic of the time. It is hardly surprising that Strauss kept his eyes firmly on the cheering audience and dismissed the sniping critic from his mind. Yet Hanslick was not alone, nor was the opposition entirely of a conservative stamp; Hugo Wolf, for one, shared Hanslick's outrage.[8] The reception history of *Zarathustra* fascinates partly because themes in the adverse reviews also surfaced with surprising effect among those who might otherwise be classed as supporters. Hanslick's review isolates, however casuistically, the main lines of criticism for the next seventy years of the work's history: the objections to the use of Nietzsche, to programmes in general, and to Strauss's powers of invention.

The review unquestionably hit its mark; Steinitzer felt obliged to counter-attack when his monograph first appeared, and he chose to focus his argument on Beethoven's Fifth Symphony in direct emulation of the offender: so understandable was *Zarathustra* as music, that one 'needs a programme for it as little as for the C minor symphony of Beethoven'.[9] Richard Specht also took issue with Hanslick and with those who knew Nietzsche only 'from hearsay'.[10] The outrage of these Strauss disciples may partly be explained by a certain sense that the opponents' criticisms had made an effect; Steinitzer by 1911 was certainly conscious of a falling-off in performances in comparison with other tone poems. Writers such as Steinitzer and Specht had a duty to oppose the Hanslickian position in the interest of revaluing what they regarded as 'the most daring of [Strauss's] symphonic works'.[11]

The controversy over Strauss's choice of a Nietzschean subject was not always principled or aesthetic. It grumbled on as a source of discord with Bayreuth. Even Strauss felt compelled to describe the work as 'notorious' to Cosima. To her credit, she replied that she heard 'praise of it from all sides', but protested 'only against poor Nietzsche as programme-poet, because sadly he has been sick, after all, for over twenty years', a venomous parenthesis that damned everything Nietzsche had written since *Menschliches, Allzumenschliches* had given offence to Wagner. To her it also seemed comical that Nietzsche had set himself up as the prophet of 'cheerful malice' (as Strauss described 'us wicked brothers in Nietzsche'), responding that he had never laughed and had seemed taken aback by Wagnerian humour; perhaps she might have thought a little longer about that.[12] Cosima represented a curious link for Strauss to the philosopher, which he must secretly have relished in spite of the strains that it imposed.

One of the main issues in the controversy between Nietzsche and Wagner had little bearing on the debate about Strauss's tone poem, however: the question of the 'Mediterraneanization' of music which Nietzsche had enthusiastically discerned in *Carmen*. Specht admittedly felt that 'Nietzsche's longing for a particular type of music' and his vision seemed 'embodied anew in Strauss', but these were the sentiments of a writer who painted aesthetic and critical issues impressionistically; most Strauss scholars have ignored this particular issue or even rejected Specht's opinion.[13] The greatest problem for most writers was the difficulty in reconciling the abstraction of a philosophical text with music (which for many others required an equal but different abstraction). The apostle of expression, Friedrich von Hausegger, remained uncertain about *Zarathustra*, even though he sensed that 'it is not so much an urge awakened by a philosophical issue, but much more the emotional content underlying it, which causes him to express himself in music.'[14] Whatever the doubts that Hausegger felt, he discriminated clearly enough the nature of Strauss's achievement. In this Hausegger was followed by others who insisted on the need to see Nietzsche only as spur to Strauss's fantasy; Oscar Bie in a much reprinted monograph insisted that Strauss set the 'Zarathustrian' and the human in direct opposition in the opening theme and the chromatic figure from bar 23, an interpretation which is a simple variation on the received wisdom about nature and the World Riddle set against the 'Sehnsucht' of humanity.[15]

Others went further and sought to sever the connection between Strauss and Nietzsche more completely. Yet those who maintained that Strauss had created in reality a piece of 'absolute music' were often also those who most needed programmatic references to explain it. Explication in such cases involved an initial denial of any real link between musician and philosopher, followed by a recourse to Nietzsche in an attempt to convey something of the work's flavour.[16] Specht himself pointed out that in places Strauss's titles and Nietzsche's aphorisms seemed at cross purposes, notably in 'Von der Wissenschaft' and 'Der Genesende' (though the latter is not the most obvious of examples); indeed, Strauss's manner was hardly as aphoristic as Nietzsche's (which may be granted with reservations), nor as rhapsodical (which requires more careful consideration). In practice, Nietzsche's aphorisms, by being themselves rhapsodical, hardly seem aphoristic in the end, hence Specht's replacement of philosophy and aphorism with 'Urgefühle' as Nietzsche's principal legacy to the musician; by insisting on such feelings, writers restored the emphasis from philosophy to the poetic.[17]

From 'basic feelings', the next stage for the defenders was to turn the content into generic characteristics, to liken the waltz rhythms not to Zarathustra's dance songs but to Beethoven's scherzos; the hope was to show that the work was 'too much and too exclusively music for its opponents'.[18] Here Strauss himself might have approved, since his comments on his own music at times did take precisely this direction; so *Till Eulenspiegel* was a rondo expanded by poetic content and resembled Beethoven's Eighth Symphony, *Don Quixote* was 'the battle of one theme against a nonentity', and *Zarathustra* was 'the alternation of the two most remote keys (the second!)'.[19] But here the opponents had virtually ceased to be those who disparaged the suitability of Nietzsche for music; the enemy was now the devotee of absolute music.

Those who sought to defend Strauss on the grounds that he had merely responded to, or even depicted, basic feelings, discovered too late that the debate had moved on. Here Hanslick set the tone of the opposition by painting Strauss as a significant step beyond Liszt. Time and again, Strauss appears in the literature on the symphonic poem not as an apostle of feeling or expression (as he saw himself), but as the narrator or illustrator. Critics who adopted such a position then felt free to comment authoritatively on the perceived content, as though reading a literary text. So Mendl, who clearly felt that Strauss lacked any qualifications to be considered poetic, noted that he dealt in 'a forceful, supple prose – and his so-called "tone-poems" are not poems at all, but rather brilliant short stories, insofar as it is possible to draw an analogy between music and literature'. Once more prose and poetic verge on value judgements, and are then taken as theoretical bases for some very confident, if eccentric pronunciations (as when Mendl notes that *Don Juan* is 'not markedly sexual').[20] Whatever the merits of this argument (and it is tempting to dismiss it as chatter masquerading as criticism), it does not question the legitimacy of programme music.

A much more forceful and negative argument was presented by Otto Klauwell in his widely influential *Geschichte der Programmusik*. In this account, Liszt, by infusing programme music with emotional content, had moved beyond the tone painting from which all programme music had set out. Strauss effectively reversed the step.[21] In this argument, however, Klauwell virtually redefined the poetic idea, since he conceded that such an idea was employed by Strauss as a basis for music. Klauwell goes a stage beyond Strauss himself in bestowing firm contours on the poetic; as a result, the idea itself is ruled beyond the confines of music's true area.[22] *Also sprach Zarathustra* is seen simply as the exemplification of its programme. Having begun his argument presumably with Hahn's booklet at his side, Klauwell refused to consider that this might merely be a poetic description of the work rather than the reverse. It becomes impossible to understand the work without the programme, an argument that goes a stage beyond Hanslick's picture of the listener who could not envisage the poetic source without the programme.[23] For Klauwell, then, the programme became a substitute for form, a means of lending coherence in the absence of musical structure, for which he was taken belatedly to task by Dahlhaus.[24]

Naturalism and Impressionism

Defenders of Strauss from such charges were in a curious historical dilemma. If they were all too aware of Strauss's position as leading exponent of the modern, they must have felt with the passage of time that the aesthetic support was starting to look rather old-fashioned. The problem perhaps was that the music of expression had a defender with feet of clay in Friedrich von Hausegger, whom even Strauss's champions tended to refrain from mentioning. Strauss undoubtedly saw in Hausegger a familiar chain of thought in his insistence on music as Nature's language of feeling, which was traced back through such familiar channels as Darwin and Herder to a distant original union of speech and music (with music seen as issuing from the former). Here too was defended Strauss's fondness for musical symbolism, which he himself brought out from time to time in his additions to Berlioz's treatise on orchestration.[25] Music became in time 'a form of imitation' that was morally ennobling as well as being rooted in nature; the rhythms and gestures of the human body became the motivation of instrumental music, rather as Wagner insisted on the dance as its essential, underlying cause. The impact of Hanslick and Schopenhauer did not substantially affect Hausegger's position, but it did undermine his credibility to the point that Paul Moos, some twenty years after Hausegger's death, could subject his theory of expression to a fairly thorough methodological drubbing, partly based on the 'naturalistic tinge' in Hausegger's thought.[26]

Naturalism was a label that was all too likely to be draped around Strauss's head as well. Even a defender such as Herwarth Walden paused here. Although he saw no further possible development for programme music, he seems to have regarded it as a form of therapy, as naturalism was for poetry, which 'compelled the artist to extreme pregnancy and destroys the concept of classical form'.[27] Hanslick would no doubt have seized gleefully on the latter point had he been alive to read it, particularly since Walden's description of Strauss as a musical rationalist conceded a certain lack of inventive power in the composer: 'the motives are created by the intellect. . . The *illustrative* is his art and strength.' Such a defence conceded rather a lot to the enemy, who could be forgiven for doubting the intellectual level displayed on the other side.

A less dangerous argument for Strauss's supporters was the view that he was an impressionist. In the hands of Oscar Bie, Impressionism was given a literary turn, as though the label had to be cleansed of 'painterly' connotations before it became safe to use. This argument cannot have been entirely pleasing to Strauss himself, however, since Bie placed him firmly in the line of Berlioz and Liszt, rather than that from Beethoven through Wagner to which he aspired. But *Zarathustra* represented a loosening of these literary ties, largely because Strauss only used titles of individual aphorisms as aids for the imagination.[28] The need to place Strauss in one of the great intellectual movements of the day became overpowering for most of his admirers, as though this would in itself refute the detractors. In this they overlooked the mirth that Hanslick was prepared to pour on Nietzsche and Ibsen in order to belittle his real target. Few thought to make the kind of argument that Jacques Barzun has applied to Berlioz, that all music is programmatic in one way or another, and that it is impossible to avoid extraneous ideas in musical activity.[29] That there could be such a thing as expressiveness, detached from representation, was only intermittently glimpsed.

The elements of this sprawling debate extended far into the history of *Also sprach Zarathustra*, colouring audience reactions consciously or unconsciously.

Even in the Zurich audiences, whose applause impressed Strauss, there were elements which reflected the doubt felt over the 'Tanzlied'.[30] There was undoubtedly a sensational side to *Zarathustra*, and this did account for the excitement engendered by the performance, but it was an excitement inspired by the 'technology', the dazzling orchestral apparatus, at least as much as by the much criticized melodic and thematic invention. The tendency was to see the themes more as symbols than as ideas in their own right, something which the guide books both fostered and sometimes deplored; this aspect has persisted as late as Gerlach's serious analytical study of Strauss's tonal structures, with themes explicitly taken as abstractions symbolizing ideas.[31] In the former German Democratic Republic, opinion inevitably took a shift in perspective, without quite abandoning the old negative tradition. Ernst Krause's view that the best of Strauss's tone poems were those which could leave their programmes behind to the point where they were virtually 'absolute music' made an exception for the 'pictorial' harmony of *Zarathustra* (a strange concept). Inevitably that work was seen as the most dated, accessible only to 'those who find the way into Nietzsche's nebulous house of ideas'. Nietzsche, Schopenhauer and Stirner hardly figured as intellectual giants in such a world-view; but altogether more bizarre was the idea that Strauss might have set out in the 'Tanzlied' 'to bring Nietzsche to the ordinary man', a task in which Krause felt he emphatically failed.[32]

Zarathustra in France: Romain Rolland and 'Neroism'

A special case in the reception history of *Also sprach Zarathustra* is provided by France. Some reactions were based on the music, such as the well-known enthusiasm of Vincent d'Indy, who acclaimed it as a masterpiece and described Strauss as 'the German composer whom I treasure most'.[33] Strauss performed it twice in Paris before the century ended, again to tumultuous applause. Even here, however, there was as much interest in the Nietzschean aspect of Strauss, concerning whom there was a certain trepidation (in spite of that respect for France and its culture that Nietzsche increasingly displayed in the latter stages of his life). Debussy expressed this concern in 1903 without any particular animus; anti-German passions were not yet as marked as in his later years:

. . . his eyes and stance are those of a 'superman', in the words of Nietzsche, a man who must have had an important influence on Strauss. He must have inherited from Nietzsche a scorn for piffling sentimentalities and also the desire that music should no longer be merely a bringer of light into our darkness, but that it should replace the sun itself. I can assure you there is plenty of sun in the music of R. Strauss . . .[34]

The last may be a conscious hint at Nietzsche's Mediterranean music (Debussy had heard *Aus Italien* in the same series of concerts), but the tone of the reference is neutral. An ideology of Strauss and the Superman emerges in French criticism with Romain Rolland, whose interpretation of Strauss, Nietzsche and *Zarathustra* is an important and distinct subsidiary strand in the work's reception.

Few French writers of the age were as interested in and open to German ideas as Rolland, to the point of incurring the enmity of many of his own countrymen. His stand against the First World War and in favour of solidarity among intellectuals of all nations was based in large measure on his confidence that a substantial body of opinion in Germany would agree with him, in which he was sadly mistaken. His comments on *Zarathustra* are not to be dismissed lightly as part of that French dream of revenge for 1871 that was one of the contributory causes to the war. Yet equally he was sensitive to nuances of political and intellectual feeling in Germany and remained critical of undemocratic tendencies in a country where democracy was tethered both constitutionally and ideologically. Rolland first met Strauss at Bayreuth in 1891 and heard *Zarathustra* soon after its first appearance when Strauss conducted it at a Lamoureux concert on 22 January 1899 (not 1898, as given in the standard edition of the Strauss-Rolland correspondence). The concert included works by Beethoven and Wagner, where Strauss's conducting verged on 'excitable and disjointed roughness', which nevertheless managed to impress Rolland in spite of a certain freakishness.[35] *Zarathustra* inspired much more doubt.

Zarathustra, which should contain all the philosophical sentiments: nature, religion, science, disgust, joy, irony, laughing lions – is obscurely complex from an intellectual point of view.

He saw vulgarity beneath the brilliant orchestral surface, and thought that reminiscences of Schumann, Mendelssohn, Wagner and Gounod (to the extent of one phrase seeming 'an unconscious parody of a tune from *Faust*') undermined the invention. The evocations of laughter impressed him more, but the historical coincidence of Nietzsche, Strauss and Kaiser Wilhelm suggested that 'there's Neroism in the air'.[36]

Beneath their friendship, there always was an element of mistrust in the relationship between Rolland and Strauss, which certain works brought out more than others. Rolland was fascinated by the contradictory impulses in Strauss's character, the mixtures of indolence and energy, courtesy and rudeness. Whereas he could afford to luxuriate in *Ein Heldenleben*, find amusement in *Don Quixote*, and write the songs off as merely sentimental, *Zarathustra* challenged him to make judgements that went beyond the musical weaknesses perceived in the work. Thus Strauss's languor and strength chimed with the transience and delirium which would sap the 'equilibrium of omnipotence' that was Nietzsche's legacy to Wilhelmine Germany.[37] This interpretation was not the product of unthinking chauvinism, since few French intellectuals knew Germany at first hand so well as Rolland. The equation of the Kaiser's posturings with Nietzsche is a curious one that takes the potentially brutal aspects of his message for the whole, and adds the seemingly obligatory reference to delirium in reminder of the awful fate which the philosopher's thinking had inflicted on his own wits. Strauss's understanding of Nietzsche seemed partial to Rolland, and he expressed the essence of Hahn's programme in as compressed a form as anyone has ever managed:

In his mind, he really did want to express, right up to the end of the symphony, the hero's inability to satisfy himself, either with religion, or science, or humour, when confronted with the enigma of nature.[38]

The deepest reason for Rolland's rejection of *Zarathustra* resided in his awareness of the anti-democratic basis of Strauss's thinking, which was directly antithetical to Rolland's own aspirations to establish an art that was not merely for the rich bourgeoisie:

When the word 'people' is mentioned, this disciple of Nietzsche understands: rabble; worse, perhaps, than the pleasure-seekers whom it wishes to destroy.[39]

The events of the war merely served to harden Rolland's antipathy to *Zarathustra* among Strauss's music (of which he preserved on the whole a favourable opinion). The judgement which he expressed in his diary for 1924, 'laughter without frenzy, the dance of the spheres reduced to a Viennese waltz', restricts itself, however, to aesthetic matters.[40]

These private opinions inevitably coloured Rolland's public utterances. In an article of June 1899, he tried to make as much of a Nietzschean out of Strauss as he could, quoting extensively from *Jenseits von Gut und Böse*, in particular the famous passage about a 'supra-German music . . . at home with big, beautiful, lonely beasts of prey', which is at once an aspect of Nietzsche's southern longings and of that writing on music of which Strauss had been so scornful in connection with this very book.[41] However appropriate this citation, it led Rolland to note the Italianate (and hence Nietzschean) qualities of the Straussian *cantilena*, which combined so strikingly with his Germanic virtues in harmony and polyphony.[42] In print, Rolland endeavoured to be fair to *Zarathustra* (excepting the commonplace qualities of some thematic material), but still allowed most of his private misgivings to infiltrate the essay. Strauss by now was probably in no mood to protest about this depiction of him as a Nietzschean, as he did earlier to Ritter and as he might have done later, when his opinion of the philosopher settled into its own equilibrium. Whether Rolland's description is an entirely fair characterization of the work, however, is doubtful. Michael Kennedy has rightly taken him to task in the person of his representative, Barbara Tuchman, whose description, however, is a wretched parody of Rolland. But Kennedy in his turn also distorts in suggesting that 'Strauss's admiration was for Nietzsche's literary prowess, not for his philosophy'.[43] The evidence is clearly there that Strauss found aspects of Nietzsche's work strongly sympathetic; we cannot turn Strauss into a believer in democracy even in English moderation. Rolland heard *Also sprach Zarathustra* as dangerous; the danger was part of its modernity, but Rolland expressed it in terms quite different from the persiflage of Hanslick. That the danger seems to have passed, leaving an orchestral superscore in place of the Superman, is a matter of history, but scrupulousness demands that the danger be accurately recorded in any account of the work.

Reappraisal: from Superman to science fiction

English-language criticism, with one notable exception, has not shown the same concern with ideas in *Zarathustra* as Rolland and Strauss's compatriots. The value of Del Mar's account resides not in a grand ideological overview, but in the specifics of musical analysis and criticism. The claim has been made that American critics tended to emphasize the Nietzschean aspect of Strauss's output as a whole in a negative way. If the view of Henry George Farmer is an accurate reflection, however, then that tradition rests on a misunderstanding much more far-reaching than anything Specht envisaged. The events of the thirties and forties, when Nietzsche's writings were twisted to ends that he would have deplored and denounced, left a residue of embarrassment among writers as late as Del Mar, who described the subject as 'particularly out of spirit with the times'.[44] Nowadays Nietzsche is the patron saint of Deconstruction, hardly a month goes by without a new addition to the

Nietzsche literature in English (often from America), and the embarrassment of the fifties lingers on mainly in the gospel according to William Rees-Mogg. In wartime, when Farmer was writing, Nietzsche was inevitably interpreted in the light of the transcripts of the notorious Leopold and Loeb murder case of 1924 (where the philosopher was widely believed to have provided the justification for a 'motiveless' crime); Farmer's article is too banal to contemplate for any great length of time. Aspects of it do suggest a *reductio ad absurdum* in advance of Peter Franklin's 'autobiographical' reading of *Zarathustra*.[45] This, however, is an approach which has gone beyond mere critique and proposes instead an alternative narrative to explain the position of the work in Strauss's career.

It is striking that the debate about *Zarathustra*'s characteristics and merits has been carried on to a large extent in literary terms, with criticism of musical aspects (usually the melodic and thematic invention) added in parenthesis. Composers, on the whole, have not devoted much time to the tone poem, as though it was swallowed rapidly in the rush of the new. The fugue theme of 'Von der Wissenschaft' eventually became part of the prehistory of the twelve-note serial idea, though the repetition of C within the very first bar of the subject, and of G in the third bar, does not make it as perfect an example of 'all the twelve notes in a self-contained form, without repetition' as Rufer imagines.[46] But it was not an example which Schoenberg himself cited, doubtless because while the theme may in abstract be 'twelve-note', its mode of development bears little resemblance to serial procedures; when the resemblance has been noted, there is little left to say, as is evident in the paucity of Rufer's comments. Its true musical influence is rather to be found in the works of *Zarathustra*'s great admirer Bartók, who left no essay dealing with it (though he wrote with great penetration of other works by Strauss). His response to the work, which he first heard at the Budapest premiere of 2 February 1902, was not limited merely to his subsequent symphonic poem *Kossuth*.[47] In 1905, his experience of *Zarathustra* still seemed a yardstick by which to judge the discovery of a new masterpiece or influence; in his case, the shock of Strauss's work may have been all the greater for (or alternatively have contributed towards) his enthusiasm for Nietzsche.[48] The most obvious homage to *Zarathustra* in Bartók's career is much later, however, in the organization of the fugue in the *Music for Strings, Percussion and Celesta*, though there the implications of Strauss's work are amplified in a more systematic manner.

Undoubtedly the biggest single factor in changing the general picture of *Zarathustra* was the appearance in 1968 of Stanley Kubrick's film, *2001 – A*

Space Odyssey. It is hard to know which was the bigger 'hit', the film or its soundtrack, which boasted further music by the younger Johann Strauss, Ligeti and Khatchaturian. The exploitation of classical music by the film industry was a long-established Hollywood tradition, though Kubrick's original intention may have been to commission a score from Alfred Hitchcock's favourite composer, Bernard Herrmann.[49] Kubrick used no more than the first twenty-one bars of Strauss's tone poem as framing music for the whole film, thereby acknowledging their curiously self-contained nature: few compositions have ever begun with so overpowering a statement of a key, to the point that they could equally well have begun or ended a piece (a trick known to numerous earlier composers, such as Mozart in the first movement Allegro of his D major String Quintet). Such popularity as Kubrick won for Strauss therefore was of a curious kind. Audiences were allowed to hear virtually all of *The Blue Danube* for a ballet of orbiting space vessels, but a mere snippet of *Zarathustra*, which nevertheless came to stand for the whole.

Kubrick took some care to build the extract into the structure of the film, underlining its importance by a third statement not long after the start. The three references mark major stages in the film's argument and are associated with visual images. Thus at the beginning, Kubrick's camera pans out from the dark side of the moon to reveal the sun rising from behind the earth, flooding it in a crescent of light that is invariably recalled with the *Zarathustra* theme. The second statement is prompted again by the sun, this time emerging over the top of a mysterious black monolith and again casting a reverse crescent of light. A key moment in the drama, the episode leads to a stage in the 'ascent' of man. His ape-like ancestors, whose vegetable existence is disturbed by the monolith, discover in the bones of a long dead body potential tools and weapons (with the violence of the latter underscored in two shots of animals falling beneath blows from the bones).

The monolith is rediscovered in the present age by astronauts on the moon, where it points towards Jupiter. As a result an expedition is mounted which discovers a larger monolith acting as a kind of star gate. In an extended fantasy, in which the spacecraft increasingly takes on the appearance of an inseminating agent penetrating a womb-like galaxy full of amoebal and reddened gaseous clouds, man consummates a mystic marriage with the stars whose issue is the star-child. His return through the gate leads to the final statement of *Zarathustra*, with the crescent now not of sunlight, but of the container in which the star-child moves, a reminder of the space helmet of the final astronaut. Whether Kubrick intended this mystical act of union to remind the viewer of the marriage of Zarathustra and Life at the close of Part III of

51

Nietzsche's book is not clear. Their child is the Eternal Recurrence, in recognition of which Zarathustra bestows the name Eternity upon Life. Kubrick leaves his film on the image of the child dwarfing the planets of the solar system. Where Nietzsche preaches recurrence and ascent towards the Superman who is associated with it, Kubrick's 'ascent' seems more Darwinian. Since Strauss also provided an evolutionary scenario for his tone poem, the link is suggestive but resistant to total integration.

Whether Kubrick's effect on the reception history of *Zarathustra* was either strong or beneficial is not without an element of controversy. Kennedy pointed out that a revival in the work's fortunes was under way before 1968, and certainly some recordings of the work had already appeared in the stereo age, including the highly influential readings by Fritz Reiner and Herbert von Karajan (his first).[50] *Zarathustra*'s revival was no doubt also influenced by the sudden rush to achieve new standards of fidelity in reproduction with the advent of stereophonic sound. Where Kubrick's film was particularly influential was not so much in the history of the work as in the independent history of the increasingly notorious and ubiquitous opening. Impressed more by the opening shot of *2001* than by its evolutionary symbolism, the BBC quickly hitched its coverage of the Apollo moon-shots to the extract, and shortly afterwards Ken Russell turned the same bars back against their creator by employing them as a rhetorical deflationary device against every negative strain in Strauss's character and career. From sunrise and World Riddle, the opening had become a mere symbol of extravagance. Here Kubrick's film had an unfortunate consequence, since the intricacy of its special effects, the supposed obscurity of its symbolism and above all the size of its budget quickly marked it down for destruction; it came to symbolize a form of meaningless Hollywood extravagance, the realization of a MacLuhan-esque nightmare, whether among those critics of film who operated with a brand of sociological critique derived from studies of Benjamin and the Frankfurt school, or among practitioners and advocates of underground cinema.[51]

The inflation of the film helped to foster the reputation for inflation of the tone poem. What displeased the academic and critic, however, did it little harm with the marketing of the LP and subsequently the CD. The detailed and sumptuous orchestration of *Zarathustra* made it an essential vehicle for the demonstration of virtually every new recording device, company or star conductor. It followed Karajan's career with almost the same regularity and frequency as cycles of Beethoven symphonies. The influence of Kubrick's film became apparent in sleeve designs, which in numerous cases took as their starting points images of planets and eclipses, thus demonstrating the work's new content. With this went a tendency to inflation in performance that took the work past the 'thirty-three ugly long minutes' which Hanslick had suffered towards the thirty-five minutes of some recent recordings.[52] But this perhaps was a general problem with recording in the age after Klemperer, Barbirolli and Karajan, where olympian wisdom could add anything up to five minutes to the time of the Adagietto of Mahler's Fifth Symphony.

More interesting is the contention made about a recent reissue of a recording by Clemens Krauss, that the difference between conductors close to Strauss's generation and those of the last twenty years could also be assessed in stylistic factors; the glamour beloved of high fidelity had replaced 'sensitivity to balance' and 'transparency of orchestral sound'; the quality of Krauss's recording, dating from 1950, is certainly sufficient to enable the listener to test the hypothesis and find it accurate enough.[53] The problem, however, affects more than *Zarathustra*, since even a witty, transparent score such as *Don Quixote* tends nowadays to have acquired a pall of glamour conspicuously absent from the readings of Strauss and Beecham. The combined effect of film and market may have revolutionized the reception of *Zarathustra*, but the problem is more wide-spread. To deplore it is probably futile. It is merely another stage in the reception of the tone poem that has taken it away from Nietzsche as far as a mass audience is concerned. When even a Straussian such as Kennedy is content to sit back and listen to it as unprogrammatic, or as *Also sprach Richard Strauss*, it has become apparent that Klauwell's belief in the necessity of Nietzsche to understanding has suffered a refutation of a kind.[54] Whether *Zarathustra* can also throw off this legacy of gigantism imposed long after the expiry of the Wilhelmine Empire remains to be seen.

6

Narratives

The tone poem as Nietzschean narrative

Given the frequency with which the label 'narrator' is applied to Strauss as tone poet, it is natural to wish to test the suitability of the concept of narration in relation to *Also sprach Zarathustra*. This immediately raises problems, since it is at best doubtful if music can be, as opposed to represent, a narrative. As Nattiez has observed, a symphonic poem cannot be translated into another medium, but 'We can summarize or translate the narrative by which the composer was inspired.'[1] In the present context, narrative is to be understood as something which goes alongside the music, a meta-narrative, with three possibilities of reconstruction. The first is to take Strauss's section headings and compare them with the corresponding sections in Nietzsche. This is already tending towards musical analysis rather than criticism, since it may be that comparisons will reflect structural similarities rather than narrative equivalencies. As an alternative, it is possible to consider Strauss's headings and their place in Arthur Hahn's programme book, which is how the question of *Zarathustra* and narrative has usually been treated. The third possibility is to retain the headings only as vague outlines in an alternative narrative, hermeneutically derived from a wider consideration of issues in the work and in other pieces by Strauss and his contemporaries. Usually such activity in Strauss criticism has involved a strong biographical element in clear response to his later explicitly autobiographical works, *Ein Heldenleben* and *Sinfonia Domestica*. There is a distinction to be made between the first approach, which assumes that the book may tell us something about the tone poem, or that the tone poem illustrates points, themes or arguments from the book, and each of the other positions, which regard the references to the section headings of the book as indications of stimulation to composition rather than content.[2]

The following list provides the eight headings included in the full score of *Also sprach Zarathustra*, together with translations, indications of their place within the tone poem, and the number of the corresponding section in Nietzsche.

'Von den Hinterweltlern' ('Of the Afterworldsmen')	bar 22; Part I, §3
'Von der grossen Sehnsucht' ('Of the Great Longing')	bar 75; Part III, §14
'Von den Freuden- und Leidenschaften' ('Of Joys and Passions')	bar 115; Part I, §5
'Das Grablied' ('The Funeral Song')	bar 164; Part II, §11
'Von der Wissenschaft' ('Of Science')	bar 201; Part IV, §15
'Der Genesende' ('The Convalescent')	bar 287; Part III, §13
'Das Tanzlied' ('The Dance Song')	bar 409; Part II, §10
'Nachtwandlerlied' ('The Night Wanderer's Song')	bar 876; Part IV, §19

A number of points is immediately apparent. The opening of the work has no title, and is generally assumed to be identical with the book's opening because of the printing of its first words as prologue to the tone poem. Nietzsche's sequence for the titles is completely discarded. Each part of the book apparently contributes two headings, but there is no pattern to the way in which they are placed. Where Strauss used headings which are adjacent in Nietzsche, e.g. 'Der Genesende' and 'Von den grossen Sehnsucht', he reversed their order and separated them by other sections.

Two section headings also cause problems. 'Das Tanzlied' has a parallel section in Part III entitled 'Das andere Tanzlied' (§15). Strauss obviously could not use a title that depended on there being two dance songs. As a result, it is hard to tell which he had in mind. It is possible that he merely wanted to emphasize the idea of dancing, and that it is unnecessary to distinguish between the two. But Strauss's 'Tanzlied' goes straight into the midnight bell's song which is first heard in Part III at the end of 'Das andere Tanzlied'. The implication is that Strauss's dance song is 'Das andere Tanzlied'. The problem was confused, however, by a passage in Arthur Hahn's programme book, where a theme from the 'Tanzlied' was designated 'Nachtlied', a title taken from Nietzsche (Part II, §9, and thus immediately preceding the first dance song). Possibly he may have been prompted to this interpretation simply by the word 'dunkel' in Strauss's short score at this point (since it is at the very least possible that Hahn knew something of Strauss's sketches); 'dark' is all that is left in the short score of the 'dark blue' brass tones of the sketches. Lest the connection be missed, Hahn quoted the opening words (used by Delius in *A Mass of Life*):

It is night: now do all leaping fountains speak louder. And my soul too is a leaping fountain.

It is night: only now do all songs of lovers awaken. And my soul too is the song of a lover.[3]

This passage provides the 'poetic mood' of Strauss's theme, which occurs at bar 629. This is typical of Hahn's approach, which mixes Strauss's titles with references to other things in Nietzsche. He makes it clear that the title refers to the C minor theme of 'Joys and Passions' in its waltz-like transformation, and notes that it mingles with 'Das Tanzlied'. It is a little unfair, therefore, for Del Mar to pillory Hahn for allowing an additional title to creep into subsequent analyses; it may equally have been the fault of Rolland, who read 'Nachtlied' for 'Nachtwandlerlied'.[4] As a section title, it has no sanction other than appearing in a programme book of which Strauss approved in general terms, and merely constitutes a piece of poeticizing to establish mood. Both dance songs take place in the evening or at night, therefore the presence of a 'Nachtlied' need not relate exclusively to either in spite of its proximity in Nietzsche to the first.

The second problem is purely a matter of confusion in the secondary literature and concerns 'Nachtwandlerlied', a section that in many editions of Nietzsche's *Also sprach Zarathustra* is entitled 'Das trunkne Lied'. Quite a few Straussians have been misled by this into noting that there was no such section in Nietzsche's book as 'Nachtwandlerlied'.[5] The general assumption in the Strauss literature has been that Nietzsche changed the title from 'Das Nachtwandlerlied' to what is usually spelled as 'Das trunkene Lied'.[6] This is also the standard view in English writing, where Del Mar claimed that Nietzsche made the change 'in the definitive version', a very odd remark, since it begs the question what the definitive version of Part IV might be: the private printing for Nietzsche's friends, or the various published versions as a separate part or in a single integral volume which appeared after Nietzsche became insane.[7] At least one authority describes 'Das trunkne Lied' as the earlier of the two titles, and the most authoritative of Nietzsche complete editions follows 'Das Nachtwandlerlied'.[8] Strauss's title, then, is founded in Nietzsche, though whether he used one or the other is irrelevant to the content of the section.

The extract from 'Zarathustras Vorrede' that Strauss placed at the head of his tone poem is:

When Zarathustra was thirty years old, he left his home and the lake of his home and went into the mountains. Here he had the enjoyment of his spirit and his solitude and he did not weary of it for ten years. But at last his heart turned – and one morning he rose with the dawn, stepped before the sun, and spoke to it thus:

Great star! What would your happiness be, if you had not those for whom you shine!

You have come up here to my cave for ten years: you would have grown weary of your light and of this journey, without me, my eagle and my serpent.

But we waited for you every morning, took from you your superfluity and blessed you for it.

Behold! I am weary of my wisdom, like a bee that has gathered too much honey; I need hands outstretched to take it.

I should like to give it away and distribute it, until the wise among men have again become happy in their folly and the poor happy in their wealth.

To that end, I must descend into the depths: as you do at evening, when you go behind the sea and bring light to the underworld too, superabundant star!

Like you, I must *go down* – as men, to whom I want to descend, call it.

So bless me then, tranquil eye, that can behold without envy even an excessive happiness!

Bless the cup that wants to overflow, that the waters may flow golden from him and bear the reflection of your joy over all the world!

Behold! This cup wants to be empty again, and Zarathustra wants to be man again.

Thus began Zarathustra's down-going.

From this famous passage, most commentators have isolated the sunrise, illustrated in the trumpet calls and C major cadence of the first twenty-one bars, as indicative of the work's feeling for nature, its relationship to landscape, though they have seldom felt the need to go further.[9] Zarathustra, who 'stepped before the sun' ('trat vor die Sonne hin'), resembles in wording that individual who enters the world in Strauss's short score ('Das Individuum tritt in die Welt'), though the change from Zarathustra to 'the individual' is significant of Strauss's move towards a more evolutionary programme.

The motivation for bringing 'Von den Hinterweltlern' into immediate proximity with the opening almost certainly stems from Zarathustra's encounter with the hermit as his first human contact in his going-down. The theme 'God is dead' is dwelt on at some length in the opening sections of the book; as a result, the illusion that Strauss is following or illustrating Nietzsche is preserved for a little while. There is some evidence that Strauss found Nietzsche's suggestive title, which plays on 'Hinterwäldlern' ('backwoodsmen'), somewhat too obscure, and he substituted 'Vom Göttlichen' ('Of the divine') for the first Cologne performance.[10] In Nietzsche's section, Zarathustra teaches that God is 'human work and human madness, like all gods!', and that heavens are the product of 'suffering and impotence'. Man should no longer 'bury [his] head in the sand of heavenly things, but . . . carry it freely, an earthly head which creates meaning for the earth!'

That the God in Strauss is specifically Christian is suggested by the reference to the chant, 'Credo in unum deum'. Strauss's short score indicates the terror of the pious as the individual appears, but quickly moves towards the portrayal of religion through hymnal textures in divided strings and organ. Short score and published score insist on 'Andacht', devotion, as the quality of this music, which has textures, tonal scheme and melodic intensity worthy of one of Strauss's songs. Strauss suggests the emotions of naive believers without obvious animus other than the quotation of the chant (which we are free to regard as purely a symbol for religion or 'palpably cynical' as Del Mar insists), leaving the context of the remainder of the tone poem to provide the implicit critique which is explicit in Nietzsche.[11]

With 'Von der grossen Sehnsucht', Strauss strikes out into the heart of the book, the gradual approach to, and exposition of, the Eternal Recurrence. In Nietzsche, Zarathustra here dispels the idea of sin 'with the storm which is called "spirit"'. Freedom and contempt replace obsequiousness, and Zarathustra's soul becomes 'superabundant and heavy'. This 'fullness looks out over raging seas'. The soul wonders whether taking is not compassion and longs to give thanks and weep; to avoid this the soul must sing 'until all seas grow still to listen to your longing', the longing of over-fullness. Strauss certainly provides a tempestuous and changeable context, but there is no equivalent to the sense of fullness that Zarathustra has bequeathed to his soul. Instead further references to 'Credo' and organ intonations of 'Magnificat' suggest that in Strauss, obsequiousness is still to be overcome. The sudden irruption of B minor at the start of the section and the upward rush of the themes to a high register may be a gesture of freedom, but further than this the listener cannot go in finding Nietzschean parallels.

By now it should be apparent that the thread of narrative derived from Nietzsche is wearing decidedly thin, and this is supported by the evidence of

'Von den Freuden- und Leidenschaften'. If Strauss derived anything from Nietzsche's section, it was the turbulence of its imagery. Nietzsche's argument here is as abstract as anything in the book, advising against the naming of virtues lest their individuality be lost in the herd. The passions of the title are those things which were once called evil but have now been 'revalued' as virtues and joys. The imagery speaks of the change of 'fierce dogs' into 'birds and sweet singers'. To have too many virtues, according to Zarathustra, is problematic, since war is a necessary result of jealousy among the virtues. But from this Zarathustra characteristically extracts a final upward turn:

Man is something that must be overcome: and for that reason you must love your virtues – for you will perish by them.

The overcoming of man is the precondition of the Superman, and is proclaimed repeatedly throughout the book. Strauss's music, by comparison, sinks downwards after the introduction of the motive of Disgust. The joys and passions of which he thinks seem to be more reminiscent of those altogether grosser emotions of *Don Juan*.

'Das Grablied' stands as a kind of pair with 'Von den Freuden- und Leidenschaften', using the same material, but constructing a different musical argument and setting it in the key of B minor. Nietzsche's section is much more narrative than any of the previous. Zarathustra travels over the sea to take 'an evergreen wreath of life' to 'the graves of my youth'. He addresses their sweet odour and turns on their murderers, who 'have cut short my eternity'. His holiest thing choked in the smoke of their piety. When he wanted to dance, they caused his favourite singer to strike up 'a gruesome, gloomy melody: alas, he trumpeted into my ears like a mournful horn!' Only his will enabled him to endure. It is his 'destroyer of all graves'.

Again the upward turn at the end is noteworthy; Zarathustra in Nietzsche asserts habitually, whereas Strauss is more intent on leading this section to a point of repose before the fugue which is to begin 'Von der Wissenschaft'. Nietzsche provides plenty of material for the musician, including the idea of a sea voyage, which can perhaps be dimly discerned in the swell of Strauss's textures. There is the juxtaposition of triumph and dance with piety and the 'mournful horn'. Strauss may have responded to this in the widely-spaced, densely scored climax in C major at bar 178, which then collapses back into B minor. As for gloomy melodies, there are certainly enough suggestions and phrases of those, and the 'mournful horn' can be seen in the melodic roles accorded to horns and cor anglais, though they are not more important than other wind instruments; the trumpet sounds only at the climax, with the

World Riddle (Ex. 1), as if to suggest that it may be the 'gruesome, gloomy melody'.

With 'Von der Wissenschaft', Strauss stepped into the curious world of Part IV. Here the essential argument of the book is over, and the main themes are discursively re-enacted by a diverse cast of 'Higher Men', behind whom real figures have been discerned, such as Wagner and Schopenhauer. The former is represented in this interpretation by a sorcerer (the Klingsor of Nietzsche's detested *Parsifal*), to whom Nietzsche opposes a 'conscientious man of the spirit', whom Hollingdale suggests might be Darwin.[12] The sorcerer ensnares the Higher Men 'in the net of his cunning and melancholy voluptuousness.' The man of the spirit attacks him and demands that Zarathustra be let in. But Zarathustra mocks the man of spirit whose virtue, science, has grown out of fear. By contrast, the Higher Men wish 'the worst, most dangerous kind of life . . . the life of wild animals, . . . the forests, caves, steep mountains, and labyrinths'. The sorcerer takes courage and claims that Zarathustra loves his enemies but takes his revenge on his friends. The Higher Men are so pleased that Zarathustra makes amends to them, though he already longs to be alone with his animals.

Strauss's depiction of science and learning in a gloomy fugue on a twelve-note theme is so famous that it is easily forgotten that the section is not co-terminous with the fugue. In the second half, fugue is brusquely thrown over with a restatement of the upward surge that began 'Von der grossen Sehnsucht', which now expands into new extensions before being checked momentarily by the themes of the World Riddle and Disgust; this check is then swept aside by a violent outburst that prepares 'Der Genesende', where the fugue resumes.

The sudden interruption of the fugue has had various interpretations. Tenschert suggested that the passage should be understood in the light of certain words in 'Von den Gelehrten' ('Of Scholars') in Part II:

I have left the house of the scholars and slammed the door behind me. Too long did my soul sit hungry at their table . . .[13]

Here again is a characteristic mode of interpretation. A narrative link can be constructed by poetic interpretation in the light of the whole book, rather than the sections isolated specifically by Strauss. Is it not also possible that the interruption might reflect Zarathustra's sudden turning on the man of the spirit? Certainly the interruption takes the most 'dangerous' form of anything in the tone poem to this point, with its high, surging violins and its giddy woodwind textures. The gloomy security of science flees before Zarathustrian laughter. Admittedly there is no sorcerer, and there is still the check in the laughter itself to be explained. Nonetheless, the structural hinge of the musical section may be discerned in Zarathustra's refutation of the scientific outlook by extolling 'adventure and joy in the unknown'.

Of all the sections in the tone poem, 'Der Genesende' seems most clearly to suggest some form of narrative, particularly if taken in connection with the second half of 'Von der Wissenschaft'. It is a curious feature of this complex that the beginning and end of 'Der Genesende' seem less structurally important and emphatic than points lying within it or within 'Von der Wissenschaft'. The start of 'Der Genesende' is admittedly the resumption of the fugue, but this pales into insignificance as a structural caesura by comparison with the monumental statement of the World Riddle theme at bar 329, the sudden plunge into B minor at bar 338, or the outburst of energy at bar 348. This constant fluctuation and the attendant sectionalization of the music's flow seem analogous to the 'events' of a narrative such as Nietzsche describes in 'Der Genesende':

Zarathustra leaps up 'like a madman', and cries out in such a voice as to terrify his attendant animals. He calls up his 'most abysmal thought' and cries out 'disgust, disgust, disgust – woe is me!' He then falls into a seven-day trance from which he rises to tell of how the monster of disgust, the 'great disgust at man', crept into his throat. But he bit its head off (thus realizing the vision that he saw in 'Vom Gesicht und Rätsel'). His animals affirm the eternity of existence. Zarathustra wonders if animals are as cruel as man, who enjoys tragedy above all things. Man revels in the sensual pleasure of penitence and sin. What is wicked in man is actually a strength. Zarathustra cried out because man's wickedness was so small. 'The little man recurs eternally.' The animals urge him to proclaim the Eternal Recurrence. When he dies, his soul will die as well, but 'the complex of causes in which I am entangled will recur – it will create me again!' He will 'tell man of the Superman once more'.

As has been noted, the theme of Disgust figures prominently at the end of 'Von der Wissenschaft', and acts as a counterpoint to the twelve-note theme once the fugue resumes. But the disgust in Strauss seems to be terror at the World Riddle, as the theme of the opening plunges the music into the chaotic groping of bars 338–47. The recovery in bar 348 on the other hand heralds the revelation of the Eternal Recurrence much more directly than the subtle dialogue between Zarathustra, his eagle and his serpent. The overcoming of disgust leads to the depiction of an almost cosmic laughter in Strauss's orchestra which is the herald of 'Das Tanzlied'.

'Das Tanzlied' in Nietzsche again has a narrative element, disguising the import of Zarathustra's meditation. One evening, Zarathustra and his disciples come upon a group of maidens dancing in a forest. When they stop on seeing him, Zarathustra urges them to dance on and sings a 'mocking-song on the Spirit of Gravity'. Wisdom tells him that love and desire are his only reasons for praising Life. Zarathustra replies that he is only fond of Wisdom 'because she very much reminds me of Life'. When Zarathustra characterizes Wisdom to Life, she replies that he is speaking of herself. Zarathustra seems 'to sink into the unfathomable' when Life opens her eyes. The dance ends, the girls depart, the sun sinks. Zarathustra wonders if it is 'not folly to go on living'. He excuses himself to his friends – 'it is evening that questions thus within me'.

In 'Das andere Tanzlied', some members of this cast are again present. Zarathustra looks into the eyes of Life then dances after her in both fear and love. Life is jealous of Zarathustra's Wisdom and tells of the midnight bell. Zarathustra (she claims) thinks of leaving her between its strokes. In answer, Zarathustra whispers something in Life's ear that causes her to marvel at his knowledge. They both weep, but 'then Life was dearer to me than all my wisdom had ever been'. The midnight bell's song sounds between the strokes, both as reminder of Death and as a hymn to eternity. The second dance song thus realizes things that were merely mocking in the first; 'the dissonance of the earlier song is resolved', and the tragic joy of life is realized in words which were set by both Mahler and Delius, but which can only be thought of in Strauss:[14]

Eins!	*One!*
O Mensch! Gib acht!	O Man! Attend!
Zwei!	*Two!*
Was spricht die tiefe Mitternacht?	What does deep midnight's voice contend?
Drei!	*Three!*
'Ich schlief, ich schlief –,	'I slept my sleep –,
Vier!	*Four!*
Aus tiefem Traum bin ich erwacht: –	'And now awake at dreaming's end: –
Fünf!	*Five!*
Die Welt ist tief,	'The world is deep,
Sechs!	*Six!*
Und tiefer als der Tag gedacht.	'Deeper than day can comprehend.

Sieben!	*Seven!*
Tief ist ihr Weh –,	'Deep is its woe –,
Acht!	*Eight!*
Lust – tiefer noch als Herzeleid:	'Joy – deeper than heart's agony:
Neun!	*Nine!*
Weh spricht: Vergeh!	'Woe says: Fade! Go!
Zehn!	*Ten!*
Doch alle Lust will Ewigkeit –,	'But all joy wants eternity –,
Elf!	*Eleven!*
– will tiefe, tiefe Ewigkeit!'	'– wants deep, deep eternity!'
Zwölf!	*Twelve!*

The listener must imagine these words, however, not in Strauss's 'Tanzlied' but at the start of 'Nachtwandlerlied'. There Zarathustra urges the Higher Men to sing the bell's song between its strokes. The two dance songs and 'Das Nachtwandlerlied' in Nietzsche thus have a clear relationship. Zarathustra, Life and Wisdom discourse in the first dance song against the background of dusk, disciples and dancing maidens. In the second, Zarathustra and Life prepare to consummate their marriage in dance; the bell's song is Life's warning of Death to Zarathustra, who, however, knows the secret of Eternal Recurrence, which he (presumably) whispers to the astonished Life. Finally, Zarathustra teaches it to the Higher Men in 'Das Nachtwandlerlied'. Strauss ran the whole complex together into one dance, whose highpoint of intoxication is also the point at which the dance begins to ebb away into a picture of eternity, coloured in ever higher statements of B major. This gradual dissipation of joy into eternity is common to Strauss, Mahler in the fourth movement of his Third Symphony, and Delius in *A Mass of Life*, though the rate of decay is slowest in Strauss, fastest in Delius, whose climax dwindles in a single bar to the quiet, protracted chords of eternity.

Strauss thus begins with a thread of Nietzschean narrative, from sunrise to the naive believers in religion, largely abandons it for hints and structural parallels in the central sections of the tone poem, but increasingly suggests a Nietzschean context from the mid-point of 'Von der Wissenschaft' to the end.[15] The appropriateness of this to his 'evolutionary' programme may be discerned in his goal of bringing the Nietzschean Superman forward as the climax of the ascent of mankind. The nearer this point approaches, the closer his music seems to the sections of Nietzsche's book, not in details but in the intended spirit. The hero of the tone poem in this view is not Zarathustra, but the individual who gradually reveals features of, and finally becomes, Nietzsche's Zarathustra. This is obviously not an illustration of Nietzsche's argument, but a borrowing of features of it to point towards a rather different programme. The Nietzschean narrative, insofar as it is recoverable from the titles, is a fragmentary overlay to another narrative, which can be described crudely as 'Dawn (of man and also the individual), encounter with nature and religion, awareness of further longings, of joys, passions and their transience in the grave, awareness and rejection of the scientific life, the overcoming of disgust at man and of man himself, and the coming of the Superman (who knows the Eternal Recurrence) in dance and song'. More than this cannot be 'illustrated' from the tone poem.

Hahn's evolutionary narrative

The account of the tone poem given by Hahn in his pamphlet is essentially a filling-out of Strauss's remarks about 'the evolution of the human race from its origin, through the various phases of development, religious as well as scientific, up to Nietzsche's idea of the Superman'.[16] Interestingly, Hahn made no reference in his account to Zarathustra's prologue, and plunged straight into sunrise and 'a great unresolved riddle'. But he did add some introductory remarks of his own, in which he provided the striking information that 'many traits in Strauss's composition' referred to Goethe's *Faust*.[17] There are certainly references to *Faust* in Nietzsche's *Also sprach Zarathustra*, notably a parody of the *Chorus mysticus* from Part II in the section, 'Von den Dichtern' ('Of Poets'). But Goethe's significance for Nietzsche lay in his perceived resemblance to the Superman himself; section 49 of 'Streifzüge eines Unzeitgemässen' ('Expeditions of an untimely man') in *Götzen-Dämmerung* (*Twilight of the Idols*; 1888/89) was devoted entirely to an appraisal of the Dionysian in Goethe. Whether *Faust*, with its Christian symbolic apparatus, was Nietzsche's favourite book by Goethe is another matter, but it is probably safe to assume that Hahn linked *Faust* as eternal striver after 'the riddle of existence' to the picture of the evolutionary ascent of mankind, probably with Strauss's approval.

The question of how far Strauss sanctioned Hahn's account is not easily answered. He was evidently prepared to allow the pamphlet to stand in lieu of the titles and the preface at early performances. Willi Schuh provides clear evidence of the trouble Strauss took in dealing with Hahn's first publisher, though this mainly concerned inadequate music examples.[18] The most compelling evidence for a degree of authority in the pamphlet, however, is the manner in which it seems to echo the sketches and short score, as if Strauss had shown some of them to him, or at least disclosed certain elements in order to keep Hahn's imagination within bounds. As a result, even where Hahn seems to go beyond the sketches, it is possible that Strauss may have given him either clues or permission to use Nietzsche as 'freely' in interpretation as he had in composing the tone poem. It is impossible not to see Strauss's hand in Hahn's insistence on thinking of the poet in Nietzsche as much as the philosopher.

Hahn's explanation starts from the opening theme as sunrise, universe and riddle. The theme in bar 23 (see Ex. 2) is mankind's 'devout terror' ('ein andachtsvoller Schauer', recalling Strauss's 'fromme Schauer') at 'the riddle of the universe'. There follow the first stirrings of 'Sehnsucht' (at bars 26 and 30), specifically the longing for knowledge, and for the solution of the World Riddle, named clearly for the first time. The names for the leitmotifs in Merian's list (see chapter 1) thus owe such validity as they possess to their derivation from Hahn's narrative (and probably therefore from Strauss and his sketches). There follows an account of man's turn to religion (without any of the cynicism attributed to Strauss by Del Mar), and of 'Von den Freuden-und Leidenschaften', which is to be more generally understood than in Nietzsche. There is another clear echo of Strauss's marginalia in the sketches when the motive of bars 95–6 is described as 'a powerful urge to life and creation' (*Lebens- und Schaffenstrieb*), which is then shortened to 'Der Lebenstrieb'. It is this which impels man into the 'joys and passions' of life, at whose climax 'the expression of passionate disgust' rings out, thus introducing the Disgust (*Ekel*) theme (see Ex. 3). 'Das Grablied' is simply a lamentation over the vanished dreams of youth (which is also Faustian, though as much in the sense of Busoni's Nietzschean Faust lamenting his vanished youth in Cracow as of Goethe's); Nietzsche's presence dwindles to a mere paragraph cited by Hahn. 'Science' then becomes a new phase in man's existence, with the fugue as the symbol of man's urge to construct systems.

The Longing motive's interruption provides release into higher spheres; at bar 251, Zarathustra finally stands before the listener, with the Disgust motive purged of its passionate character to become the beginning of convalescence. Zarathustra reflects on his past at bar 278, pours scorn on learning's fugue (in the horn figure of bar 304), only to sink down 'crushed' (*zerschmettert*) in the face of the reassertion of the World Riddle at bars 329–38. The word 'zerschmettert' indeed stands over bar 338 in Strauss's short score, but more striking are bars 329–36, which Hahn claimed remembered Faust and the Earth-Spirit more than Nietzsche. Here the association of ideas is particularly rich, since Zarathustra is equated with Faustian man, and the World Riddle becomes the Earth-Spirit, whom Faust conjures up. He further presumes to describe himself to the Spirit as 'deinesgleichen' ('your likeness'). The Spirit's response is added by Strauss at this point in his short score: 'Du gleichst dem Geist, den du begreifst, nicht mir!' ('You resemble the spirit whom you imagine, not me!'). This is a particularly crushing moment for Faust (whose collapse is described by Goethe as 'zusammenstürzend' rather than 'zerschmettert'), and the Spirit disappears, never to be recalled. The indifference of the Earth-Spirit appears as absolute as the insolubility of the World Riddle.

Zarathustra's collapse is followed by his renewed upsurge, from which point onwards Hahn's commentary is fashioned out of Nietzschean parallels and quotations. Zarathustra mocks the 'spirit of gravity' (bar 362) with recollections of the section 'Vom Lesen und Schreiben' ('Of reading and writing'); the trumpet's call, likened by most commentators to a cock-crow and described by Hahn as a 'Weckruf' ('reveille'), is the 'dancing star' of Zarathustra's prologue.[19] Disgust is overcome in laughter (with Strauss's annotation, 'grosses Lachen', over the equivalent of bar 386 in the short score as a clue). 'Das Tanzlied' is described in words from 'Die sieben Siegel' ('The Seven Seals'), the section in Nietzsche which follows 'Das andere Tanzlied'. From here on, Hahn's narrative is virtually Nietzschean, with the C major appearance of Longing (bar 737) hinting at Nietzsche's 'Ja- und Amen-Lied' ('Song of Yea and Amen'), the alternative title of 'Die sieben Siegel', whose connection with 'Das Nachtwandlerlied' is the song of the bell.

The famous ending with C major and B major placed in apparently unresolvable dissonance, is interpreted not as Eternal Recurrence but as the inability of Zarathustra to solve the World Riddle; the tone poem ends not with a solution but with a question mark. This is not necessarily a denial of the Nietzschean celebration of eternity, since the Eternal Recurrence implies the return of all problems; only the idea of Recurrence itself, which the Superman accepts, is important. A more comprehensive view of the ending than Hahn's is provided by Seidl, who read it as the opposition of Man and Superman (who is synonymous with the Recurrence).[20] Strauss's conclusion clearly is not the gesture of affirmation that Delius placed at the close of the *Mass of Life*, but rather resembles the uncertainty of Mahler's Nietzsche setting in the Third Symphony (after which Mahler steered his work towards the metaphysics that Nietzsche had slain in *Menschliches, Allzumenschliches*). Hahn's interpretation thus accords with the critique presented above of a Nietzschean narrative, since it provides Nietzschean parallels most strongly from the point at which Zarathustra appears in mankind's evolution. The correspondence with Strauss's short score and sketches is a matter of common terms for motives, and the relevance of the Faustian parallel. There is enough in this to wonder if Del Mar was justified in accusing Hahn of interpreting 'rather too freely' from Nietzsche.[21] A more grave charge might be the naivety of the language in which Hahn expressed his programme. Certainly it provided plenty of evidence for Klauwell's argument that the work simply expressed the programme. The 'free' interpretation of Hahn might arguably be said to express the spirit rather than the details in which Strauss followed Nietzsche. And Klauwell was quite prepared to do the same thing, as when he cited some words of Zarathustra about disgust when describing its theme.[22]

Strauss as Zarathustra

In both interpretations, Zarathustra evolves from the individual who is humanity. But just as Zarathustra has often been taken as equivalent to Nietzsche himself (not without reason), so there has always been a strain of criticism which has seen the 'hero' of the tone poem as Strauss. The urge to provide an autobiographical strand to interpretation had always figured strongly in writings about programme music and the New German School. Friedrich von Hausegger, for instance, took the mystical nature of Liszt's performance as an indicator of the degree to which Liszt became his own programme when he composed absolute music.[23] The most consistently expressed statement of the autobiographical strain in *Zarathustra* is provided by Peter Franklin, in what is an overt attempt at revaluation. This is intended not as a programme, but as something closer to a critique from within the music. It is also aimed against the interpretation that goes back to Hahn, viewed by Franklin as almost certainly untrue to Strauss's intentions. Here, the probability is that Franklin is in error, but that does not deny the validity of his essay as interpretation. When he attacks the view that equates the opening simply with a sunrise, it is legitimate to reply that not all interpretations do take the opening as only a sunrise (not even Kubrick's); but Franklin also has little time for the un-Nietzschean concept of what Seidl called 'the stupid "solution of the World Riddle" '.[24] Franklin's theory is more concerned with seeing *Zarathustra* in the same line as *Don Juan* and *Till Eulenspiegel*, reading each 'hero' in turn as one more manifestation of Strauss himself.[25] This rather depends on the view that Strauss must always be identified with his own creations, a claim that may be valid for some creators, but which is intolerable as a general aesthetic statement, particularly for opera and drama. To find a dramatic spokesman for the composer is frequently an object of Franklin's criticism, particularly when he writes about opera. The question remains, how dependable is the view that equates the individual who becomes Zarathustra and his Superman with Strauss himself.

In Franklin's narrative, the stages of man's evolution become soul states in a spiritual journey into 'the very much darker and profounder regions of late nineteenth-century artistic motivation'.[26] In this reading, specifically Nietzschean connotations are presented as subsidiary to the main theme, 'heroic assertion and self-discovery', a specifically Beethovenian myth that has continued to dog criticism of *Zarathustra* since the Fifth Symphony was included in the Viennese programme heard by Hanslick. The Faustian climax of 'Der Genesende' is interpreted as the overcoming of Schopenhauerian disgust, the Nietzschean realization that the Will which Schopenhauer sought to deny is 'the essential Will to all Life'; curiously, Franklin does not say 'Will to Power', the characteristically Nietzschean formula which helps to define the Superman.[27] A curious situation thus arises. Strauss is substituted for Zarathustra as hero, but at the climax, Nietzsche is substituted for Strauss. The problem is related to the manner in which other interpretations, most notably Hahn's, find Nietzsche particularly indispensable from 'Der Genesende' onwards. The interpretations that insist on 'Also sprach Richard Strauss' either use it as an aesthetic commentary (rather than interpretative narrative) independent of programmatic considerations (like Specht), are forced to equate Strauss's view ultimately with Nietzsche's (like Franklin), or use it as a means of escaping into a manner of reception characteristic of absolute music (like Kennedy).[28]

Finally, the motive that seems to be more than a sunrise, the opening trumpet call, comes to be the reflection of the Will itself, but it becomes a Schopenhauerian Will caught up in a Nietzschean adventure with Strauss as hero. Perhaps an inevitable reaction is to say that such drastically simplified pictures are the inevitable consequence of attempting to read a tone poem as though it really were a narrative, as though it really could contain a critique. But they seem an accurate enough reflection of the way in which Strauss created an essentially personal work out of a melange of influences, in which Schopenhauer should no more be discounted than Nietzsche. Franklin's reading may be tendentious, but it isolates issues in the tone poem more acutely than the sterile squabble over whether the work illustrates this or that narrative. The narratives help to illuminate the work from several different points of view, but they do not have an exclusive hold over Strauss's music. To Nietzschean, evolutionary and 'heroic' programmes inevitably must be added the structural programmes arising from considering the work as Steinitzer, Bie and Kennedy desired, as self-sufficient music.

As support for this may again be cited the song of the bell. In a narrative context, the incomparable superiority of the bell settings of Mahler and Delius over that of Strauss is incontestable. The prolonged double pedal, the echoing bell tones in the brass, woodwind and harps, and the lonely ecstasy of joy in eternity seem in Mahler a most imaginative interpretation of Nietzsche's vision, albeit one drawn into a particularly Mahlerian view of Nature that is also subsequently qualified by a naive picture of celebrating angels. With Delius, the claims of eternity become a slow procession into the infinite; the tone rises incessantly towards the jubilation of the final pages. The emphasis is on the night-wandering of Zarathustra and the Higher Men to hear the bell's song; the wandering implicitly is a programme for life and the eternally recurring circumstances of life. How much more impoverished is the bell in Strauss: twelve strokes of a (hopefully) real bell, with descending chromatic progressions in which the theme of Disgust is compelled to dance towards the vision of eternity. In any comparative assessment, Strauss's inadequacy is apparent, but only as long as Nietzsche's words remain the principal criterion. For the moments in Delius and Mahler are almost self-sufficient, whereas Strauss paints a musical transition, a unit in a structural process more complex and more 'absolute' than the others. It is a kind of yard-stick of the degree to which the narratives may be said to be something parallel to, but not intrinsically of, the tone poem. The programmatic strand is the bell itself; but the bell 'explains' the music as much through being a pedal note as through being a bell.

7

Structures

Strauss and the leitmotif

Broadly speaking, three views of structure in *Also sprach Zarathustra* have been put forward with varying degrees of rigour and subtlety, founded respectively on motivic-thematic factors independent of exact formal structures, on themes in a variation context, and on the idea of the symphony. What may be slightly surprising is the degree to which tonality has been taken as the ally not of the symphonic view, but of those who have argued for some kind of dramatic form with leitmotifs. That the whole work pivots round the antithesis of C and B is beyond dispute, having a firm grounding in Strauss's own comments. Problems immediately occur when the question of the ascendancy of one or the other arises, however, since Strauss never quite settles on either as the tonic, keeping both fairly constantly in play. Thus both keys are heard in the first thirty-four bars, with C rather the stronger. As if in compensation, the closing pages again feature both keys, with B now clearly stronger. If this famous ending is looked at with any degree of analytical rigour, it must be doubted whether C is present as a key in any meaningful sense. The chord, C–E–F♯, which Strauss places over the theme of the World Riddle or universe (bars 980–2), resolves with little effort into B major (Ex. 7a).

To describe this ending as bitonal is rather like saying that the ending of Liszt's B minor Sonata is potentially bitonal. It is possible that Liszt's conclusion was at the back of Strauss's mind when he wrote his notorious ending. In Liszt, the Phrygian second of B is used as a delaying factor, over which the upper parts resolve triads of A minor and F major (with their common C) into B major; the C in the bass is only resolved on to B after a long pause on B major (Ex. 7b). Had Strauss concluded by taking C down to B, there would not have been a quiver of surprise. The presence of G in the universal theme makes no real difference to the harmonic direction of the ending, save in a symbolic sense. The controversy about the ending is not about dissonance treatment, for Strauss does everything in an orthodox way

Ex. 7a *Also sprach Zarathustra*, bars 979–87

Ex. 7b Liszt, Sonata in B minor, conclusion

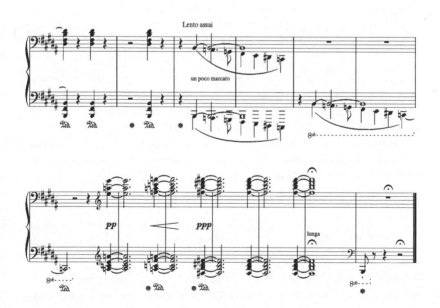

except for not providing the resolution of C; clearly this was motivated with an expressive or structural factor in mind.[1]

To say that the ending is bitonal requires a rather different view of structure than is the norm in music analysis nowadays. The growth in importance of methods of analysis founded upon the writings of Heinrich Schenker has thrown the weight of musicological opinion behind a monotonal view of music in which the Fundamental Structure (*Ursatz*) takes the polarity of tonic and dominant as the central principle of an organic view of musical form and process. In a work where two keys as far apart (in the tonal circle) as C and B form opposed structural poles, the *Ursatz* dwindles to purely local significance. A curious situation arises: the basis of structure in the whole (C and B) differs from that in the local sections (where traditional tonal schemes largely remain unchallenged), thereby leaving the notion of musical organicism irredeemably fractured. Even amongst analysts who have resisted Schenker, a similar viewpoint may be seen, as in the writings of Reinhard Gerlach: 'If there is no unequivocal "tonality" of the work, there is also no longer an unequivocal (harmonic) form.' Gerlach's solution to the problem inherent in this situation is one of the most interesting, if contentious, statements about *Zarathustra*'s structure, which is viewed as a development of an idea first seen in *Tod und Verklärung*: it is a double composition with two tonalities, in which the leitmotif (viewed challengingly as 'the forerunner of the note-row') ensures coherence. The ending is not a close in any tonal sense, but an extension into some unforeseeable perspective.[2]

Tonality and leitmotif are thus linked, but not all analysts have used a perspective quite like that of Gerlach. There are clear differences among interpretations of the manner in which leitmotifs function in *Zarathustra*, which can be discerned in his characterization of the leitmotif as a forerunner of the row. The conflict comes down to whether leitmotifs organize because they denote ideas or because they are transformed. But additionally, the idea of denotatory leitmotifs raises the question of whether the two main tonalities are not themselves leitmotifs, or leading-tonalities. The keys therefore contribute towards an associative rather than structural basis for form in the whole, while retaining their capacity for more orthodox organization at the level of sections.

It is easier to answer the question, from where did the leitmotif come, than to offer a firm definition of the term. That it is operatic in derivation is unquestioned, even if there could be discussion as to the extent to which Wagner's practice constitutes a more symphonic procedure than the more simply denotatory motives seen in Weber, his German contemporaries and successors, and his French predecessors. Among the works of Strauss and his contemporaries, there are numerous instances of a leading motive expanding to the length of a full musical period (seen at its most extreme in the operas of Pfitzner and Berg, where the term *Leitsektion* has been used).[3] That many of Strauss's themes in *Also sprach Zarathustra* are of a short, lapidary character, as Schmalz observed, helps in gaining acceptance of them as leitmotifs;[4] but the length of the A flat and C minor melodies of 'Von den Hinterweltlern' and 'Von den Freuden- und Leidenschaften' does not automatically bar them from being looked at in this light. Nonetheless, it is more likely that such extended melodies will be truncated to produce something more acceptable as leitmotif, thereby also creating the impression of symphonic fragmentation and development, or will be transformed in a Lisztian manner, thereby producing the appearance of variation procedures.

The paradox of *Zarathustra* resides in the manner in which the notion of leitmotif proves remarkably accommodating to virtually all standpoints on form. This may be because the leitmotif as such is not, in spite of Gerlach's large claim, structural in itself, but rather a unit in more all-embracing schemata. Here Arno Forchert has made some telling remarks about Strauss's procedures in *Ein Heldenleben*. Although there is 'a multiplicity of ideas of highly varied character from common motivic material', they do not form the work's musical logic. They do not, for instance, exhibit the kind of cohesion suggested by a phrase such as Schoenberg's 'developing variation'; 'rather they resemble an arsenal' of material, with a psychological explanation for their occurrence.[5] Such an approach already sees the opera composer in the Straussian tone poem.

The leitmotif thus has a psychological significance in *Ein Heldenleben*, and the interpretation is extendable to *Zarathustra* insofar as that too boasts its 'hero', be he individual, Superman or Strauss. But doubts arose in the minds of analysts shortly after the work's appearance. As early as 1899, Hans Merian was promulgating the view that Strauss had transferred the leitmotif from the music drama to the tone poem (a programme which has its theoretical justification in the letter to Thuille cited in chapter 2); but he rebelled against superficial readings that failed to note their role in the musical process.[6] A problem thus arose which has been isolated by Derrick Puffett in the case of *Salome*. Commentators, most strikingly Strauss himself in his sketches, seem to equate leitmotifs crudely with single characters or ideas: the motifs are their labels.[7] Puffett suggests that this does not actually square with Strauss's musical practice, which provided a continuum of meaning for leitmotifs, dependent on a host of changing musical, literary and dramatic contexts. This is clearly acceptable for an opera, but for an instrumental work such a continuum is not so easily established.

Nonetheless, Puffett's idea probably holds good in *Zarathustra* also, most notably in the transformation of the motive of Dread from minor to major for Faith. The opening idea already carries a continuum of meaning: nature, universe and the riddle of understanding the cosmos. That it is incorporated as accompaniment into 'Das Tanzlied' suggests the cosmic scale of Zarathustra's liberating laughter. There is evidence enough of an evolving process here, though once more it seems dependent upon reading the music in conjunction with one or other narrative. It is arguable that the real idea behind *Zarathustra* resides in this one example, for there is hardly a motive from the first part of the work that is not caught up into the dance. All the ideas of the ascent of mankind are gradually imbued with the spirit of the Superman, and the cosmos dances in the manner that Mahler also wanted to capture in waltz-time (in the scherzo of his Fifth Symphony).

Once the idea of leitmotif had taken hold, it quickly became the staple of commentators, who were left to agree or disagree with the motives that Merian singled out.[8] But his argument was directed at least as much towards musical as programmatic factors. The first two motives (Exx. 1 and 2) were conspicuous for their arpeggiated incipits which strengthened Merian's view that the rival tonalities were employed motivically – they were embedded in the leitmotifs. He stressed that these motives tended to stay in their own keys, though where transposition occurred it might have a specific meaning. Thus the transpositions of the fugue subject (which begins with the C major motive of Nature or the World Riddle) suggest different scholarly and scientific systems to explain the riddle of world and nature. The motive of Disgust in Merian's view had no tonality but began with the tritone (F–B) as a symbol of the unnatural; it thus became appropriate for the Faustian 'spirit that always denies' (Goethe's devil), and for 'the serpent of nausea that creeps into Zarathustra's mouth and whose head he then bites off'. This is not the only instance in the literature of the Disgust motive being regarded as tonally uncertain.[9] Of course, Merian also meant that the motive has no tonality of its own (like C or B), but it is impossible to accept the view that the motive tends towards the atonal, if only because the offending tritone clearly constitutes the leading-note and seventh over the dominant in C, the key in which it first appears. Just as with the ending, this apparently radical motive is easily explained in tonal terms (though it contains disruptive features); there is, however, a further symbolic level which points to something more ambiguous. Merian's equation of motive and key thus seems to refute in advance the tentative suggestion of Tethys Carpenter that *Zarathustra* is an exception among Strauss's work in that it may transform its themes tonally.[10] Merian thought of Strauss's leitmotifs as 'parallels in tones' to Nietzsche's ideas; he had no wish to view the tone poem as a translation of a literary original, though he seemed to come close to the view that to be a 'Zarathustrian' would guarantee keener insight into the tone poem.[11] The problem was that the concept 'leitmotif' immediately demanded a psychological context. Unquestionably such an interpretation accorded well with Strauss's desire to shape themes as 'characters' in a human drama. The legacy of his ruminations on this and on Liszt's over-extended developments was that developments became almost as short as themes; the pattern of *Zarathustra* at times is almost equatable with a series of themes, linked by short developmental transitions. Where the themes conform to traditional patterns of musical closure or exhibit self-contained formal characteristics, then *Zarathustra* conforms most closely to the nesting of small forms that Alfred Lorenz saw in its predecessor, *Till Eulenspiegel*.[12] The type of structure described by Lorenz is derived from the patterns of small forms and units that he analysed in Wagner's mature music dramas. The impression that Strauss's later tone poems functioned in ways related to opera with leitmotifs as cement is strengthened by such an approach.

Symphonic characteristics of *Also sprach Zarathustra*

This viewpoint corresponds only to the dramatic aspect of the tone poem; that there was another viewpoint was also emphasized by Strauss's comments on the first two movements of Liszt's *Faust-Symphonie*. In this respect, the unity of image characteristic of the Lisztian symphonic poem traditionally produced formal structures of a clarity reminiscent of the symphony or the overture. A whole school of analytical thought has sought to uncover a veiled symphony in *Zarathustra*. Admittedly, much of this has tended to resort to concepts such as 'free symphonic fantasy', as if to emphasize the gulf separating the tone poem from 'absolute' symphonies.[13] Where the central formal concept is treated freely, there can be no surprise that the various sub-categories of the symphony and sonata form are treated with similar licence. Most analyses that cling to the notion of the symphony tend to be partial, and essentially sectional. Certain points of division occur again and again, but equally there are divergences in description and emphasis. Thus Steinitzer treats the tone poem as if it were an example of a Lisztian symphonic poem in which four movements were run into a single unit; it has two subjects (the Nature and

Longing motives), a slow movement, a scherzo and a finale.[14] The slow movement is displaced in this account, comprising the A flat section in 'Von den Hinterweltlern', and taking the place of what might otherwise have been called an introduction. This is typical of many approaches; the sections of sonata form are regarded as mobiles which can be moved to new sites, while retaining some essence that is implicitly based on generic characteristics.

Steinitzer anticipates the somewhat later desire of German musicologists to discern a form of decipherable code in expressive characteristics, to the point that some sort of *Musiksprache* emerges. 'Musical language' in this context is something compounded of affect (which looks as far back as the Baroque period for rhetorical figures), historical residue (which isolates 'masculine' and 'feminine' subject groups, or codas as apotheoses from their original contexts) and key characteristics; specific parallels are usually cited as though they convey a particular content, as when Steinitzer compares the dance rhythms in *Zarathustra* with Beethovenian scherzos.[15] From this, an alternative content to the Nietzschean titles may be inferred, though Steinitzer remains content with suggestions, designed as much to refute the criticisms of Hanslick as to explain the work.

The most consistent statement of this point of view (which also forms part of the basis of Adorno's celebrated critique of Mahler)[16] is again provided by Arno Forchert, who makes explicit the picture of Strauss's endeavouring 'to bring to speech the differentiated functional characters which had been cultivated in first movement sonata form' to an even greater degree than Mahler.[17] Characteristics become 'means of representation', which is far from an unalloyed positive in Forchert's view. In the process of turning developments into 'battles', codas into havens of peace and security, structure dissociates into sections. Most of Strauss's tone poems are essentially composed from the same group of functional characteristics. Thus 'Von der grossen Sehnsucht' is a typical transition in that it embodies 'a state of suspension, indecision or transitoriness'. A historical process weakens the development, 'as the specific technique of the successive breaking-down of complex shapes originally linked to the concept of development yields to a motivic-contrapuntal process that already presupposes the dissociation of thematic shapes'. In *Zarathustra*, 'the free sectional division' turns sonata form from a schema into an ideal type.

Forchert presents ideas for an analysis, but what such an analysis might look like is suggested by Dahlhaus's brief overview of *Tod und Verklärung*. The principles are relatively few: displacement of traditional sections of sonata form, distortion of their proportions, and metamorphosis of sections into potentially independent movements. The distortion of temporal proportions (on which Dahlhaus places perhaps disproportionate emphasis) is such as to render traditional labels inadequate. Yet Dahlhaus remains convinced that such a view of form is 'nonschematic without being arbitrary'.[18] The example of *Tod und Verklärung* is well-chosen to fit the argument, inasmuch as introduction, theme groups and development do follow one another more or less in the 'proper' sequence, regardless of their proportions. This is not so obvious in the case of *Also sprach Zarathustra*, though there have been enough suggestions to enable some sort of pattern to be established. In the following overview, an attempt will be made to consider how far characteristics may be said to establish formal categories; one feature may be noted in advance, the haphazard manner in which formal events coincide with Strauss's section headings.

If the first thirty-four bars possess any traditional character at all, they may be defined as introduction acting as exposition of motives. This distinguishes them generically from an exposition with its theme groups. The three motives of Nature, Dread and Longing define or suggest three tonalities with varying degrees of clarity. The manner in which C, F minor and B minor are related and connected is superficially haphazard, though (as will be demonstrated in the next chapter) entirely at one with Strauss's stylistic practice. This type of introductory exposition of motives is familiar enough in nineteenth-century music, the first seventeen bars of Liszt's B minor Sonata being a possible parallel. The motivic units of theme groups are set out with dividing silences and drastic contrasts of texture. 'Von den Hinterweltlern' begins at the point when a change of texture and modality occurs. This may reflect a stage in the programme, but in terms of characteristics it is no more structurally important than the division at bar 35.

With the entry of the strings and organ, a typical Straussian *cantilena* starts up which immediately replaces textural discontinuity and motivic independence with a thirty-two-bar melodic paragraph. Quadratic phrasing is the unbending rule in this section, as is homophony. Tonal unity is preserved from the start until the wide-spread cadence at bar 66. Although the modulation scheme is typically Straussian in its side-slips and use of six-fours to approach new keys, it is a fairly simple structure. In outline, three sections may be discerned, four bars in A flat, twenty in a modulatory cycle, and a concluding pair of four-bar phrases which repeat the cadential pattern of the first four bars (chords I–IV–V–I). Ternary in itself, the section is redolent of the first part of some larger ternary-form slow movement, which is not completed. The hymnal textures remind Gerlach of Mendelssohn, and he

Ex. 8 bars 239–44

envisages Strauss as a time-traveller reviewing the styles of the nineteenth century (thus giving a positive slant to Rolland's suspicions of plagiarism).[19]

As has been seen, Forchert regards 'Von der grossen Sehnsucht' as something transitional, as a developmental link. Here for the first time analysis of characteristics and programmatic structure coincide. Yet it is not so 'transitional' as casual inspection suggests, for here is the first harmonized statement of the Longing motive with its characteristic extension in thirds (Ex. 8). Forchert's label fits well enough once this is past, however, and the mode of development is Strauss's favourite contrapuntal combination of short motives. There is a large-scale tonal motion (which is partly adapted from the previous section), carrying the music from B to the dominant of C.

With the arrival of C minor at the start of 'Von den Freuden- und Leidenschaften', the music reaches something which Edward Murphy describes as 'the *allegro* section', containing 'the true first-theme area of a symphony movement'.[20] In this, he follows the argument from characteristics viewed as historical residue. The equation of C minor with a certain kind of 'storm and stress' first subject recalls the almost inevitable Beethoven parallel, though it would be more interesting to consider it in relation to the corresponding section in *Tod und Verklärung*, set in the same key. Whereas Strauss there built his subject group out of 'conflict' motives and inchoate stirrings in the bass which rose to a spasmodic orchestral tutti, 'Von den Freuden- und Leidenschaften' creates an illusion of continuous melody almost as dependent on quadratic phrasing as 'Von den Hinterweltlern'. It is an illusion, inasmuch as a single voice (first violins) does sprout cadential overlaps and extensions in other parts. The most decisive of these moments

Ex. 9 bars 201–5, Fugue subject

of pseudo-polyphony is the introduction of Disgust in the trombones, which for a moment lead an ensemble hitherto dominated by string tone. The quadratic phrasing is disturbed more frequently than in 'Von den Hinterweltlern', but no more than is Strauss's wont, and the piling of Pelion upon Ossa at the cadence is hardly less characteristic. The significance of this design, which is again ternary (and follows the typical harmonic structure of the minor mode, I–III–V–I), is that it becomes a model for a song in the next section. It functions perfectly well as a short song form itself (excluding the final linking decline into B minor). The characteristics of sonata form in this section are a matter of expression and rhetoric, not form.

Perhaps the same factors turn 'Das Grablied' into a second subject. It looks, however, more like the model for future Straussian second subject areas rather than a recognizable descendant of anything in *Macbeth*, *Don Juan* or *Tod und Verklärung*. This is a function of its textural density, which anticipates the extended love scene at Fig. 32 of *Ein Heldenleben*. To read it as a second subject has the merit of placing the first subject of Murphy's standard Allegro in one of the two main keys and the second subject in the other, though Strauss rather skilfully contrives to avoid a tonic presentation of B minor in its root position. Such an interpretation, however, seems dangerously close to imposing a traditional pattern upon the work in defiance of all Strauss's strictures on traditional absolute music.

For its first thirty-eight bars, 'Von der Wissenschaft' allows no possible misunderstanding as to its genre: it is clearly a fugue. But it also develops, inasmuch as its head motive is the Nature motive, which on occasions detaches itself from the complete subject (Ex. 9). A fugue as a development is not unknown in the literature of the symphonic poem and programme symphony. 'Mephistopheles' in Liszt's *Faust-Symphonie* uses fugato (an example with precedents in Viennese Classicism and Berlioz which led in turn to countless fugatos in nationalist and programmatic symphonies). Possibly by something more than happy coincidence, one of the two symphonic poems that shared the programme on the occasion of *Zarathustra*'s première included one of the most extended fugues in the genre. Liszt's *Prometheus* contains a fugue which has aroused a certain amount of interpretative comment. The theory that Liszt chose fugal writing at this point to represent Prometheus's brother, Epimetheus, derives from Lina Ramann's much debated biography, whose final volume appeared in 1894.[21] No documentary evidence seems to exist to prove this theory, which depends upon the traditional view of Epimetheus's character: not only was he the feckless husband of Pandora, his name also signified 'afterthought', as opposed to his brother's 'forethought'. The old-fashioned form of fugue was thus appropriate as a symbol of wisdom after the event.

Although it is impossible to tell at present if Strauss knew of this story (and as a former resident of Weimar he was well placed to know both the story and the biography), his own practice seems to reflect something of this stylistic conceit. For the two fugal sections of *Zarathustra* seem designed to reflect antique and modern styles. His fugue subject is of course drastically different from Liszt's, from which a tonal answer is derived. Strauss's subject, by permitting a real answer and moving to the dominant, engenders a radical tonal scheme which climbs through the cycle of fifths to A. A couple of truncated entries on E (bars 217 and 219) link to a further entry on B with subsequent abbreviated entries on F♯ (bars 231–5). The scheme therefore carries the music from C to its opposite pole, one means of demonstrating the link between C and B, since F♯ major is the dominant of B. The anticipation of Bartók's scheme in *Music for Strings, Percussion and Celesta* is close enough, though Bartók works with two cycles of fifths, one ascending and one descending (and requires subject and answer to bring the full chromatic spectrum into play). But if the key scheme is radical, then other features seem designed to emphasize traditional procedures, notably the use of augmentation, significantly reserved for the entry on B (bar 223), partial strettos, a regular countersubject, and textures that maintain the close-knit, rhythmically homogeneous character of a baroque vocal fugue. Liszt's fugue in *Prometheus* is a much more extrovert 'modern' affair, with motivic contrasts in varied orchestral colours at least as prominent as traditional counterpoint.

The resumption of the fugue in 'Der Genesende' is also the resumption of the cycle of fifths, beginning on E and reaching C♯. From here on, however, full and abbreviated entries occur on D (bar 303), then E♭, G and B (the characteristic late-nineteenth century cycle of major thirds) before splintering into chromatic sequential writing. The regular countersubject is replaced by a constantly changing array of motives (in which Disgust is sometimes prominent), and fragmentation of the subject is more common than stretto and augmentation. The illusion of symphonic development is correspondingly stronger, and this suggests that while old-fashioned counterpoint was deemed suitable for the scientific outlook, modern orchestral developmental counterpoint, Strauss's particular strength in the first period of his career extending up to *Der Rosenkavalier*, was regarded as the natural idiom for the convalescent Zarathustra as he warred with disgust at humanity. The section that connects the two fugal passages again falls within the bounds of the species of developmental link observed in 'Von den Freuden- und Leidenschaften'. The various developmental sections thus take on 'characters' from generic associations, which also help to split the music into a kind of ternary structure: fugue, episodic link, fugue. Only the first and third of these divisions coincide precisely with Strauss's headings.

The next significant event, the recall of the Nature theme at bar 329, also fails to coincide with a Nietzschean heading. The precise status of this monumental statement, possibly the loudest moment in the work, is a complex matter. For Specht, it is (in spite of its apparent finality) the beginning of a transition to a reprise, though Murphy places this 'retransition' later in bars 348–408.[22] The confusion is in its way a valid critical reaction, since the textures in this area of the work are as discontinuous as at the opening, so much so as to suggest the complex of bars 329–47 as a varied reprise of the work's introduction, with trumpet fanfare now in full orchestra, and the original responses (bars 6, 10 and 14) relegated to low wind in bars 342–3 and 347. As in the introduction, the Longing theme then enters. But the idea of a retransition is at least as valid, partly because the whole fragmented section settles down eventually on the dominant of C (Fig. 23) in preparation for 'Das Tanzlied'.

At this point, scherzo and recapitulation seem to fuse, as if in anticipation of Sibelius's formal experiment in the opening movement of his Fifth Symphony. Writers from Specht to (most recently) Denis Wilde want to regard this as a species of transformed reprise.[23] This is hardly a point-by-point relationship, however, even if the Nature theme appears in trumpet and oboes while the solo violin weaves its spell from the salon. Rather, Strauss draws most of the earlier motives into a pattern of transformations. Thus the first violin entry (Ex. 10a) fuses elements of Longing (x) and Dread (y), changing mode and compass but retaining elements of their contours; the Dread theme becomes the second strain of the waltz (Ex. 10b); the Life-urge theme is used with minimal change in contour and function as a linking figure in the bass; and the high motive at Zarathustra's entry in Hahn's narrative (bar 251) becomes the dominant material of the next section of the waltz. The

Ex. 10a bars 428–31

Ex. 10b bars 469–76

melodic statement of 'Von den Freuden- und Leidenschaften' and the Longing theme (apart from bass entries after bar 564) are reserved, the former to constitute the A flat trio (Hahn's 'Nachtlied'), the latter to mark the resumption and final crescendo of the waltz (Hahn's 'Ja- und Amen-Lied') (Ex. 11), a particularly striking transformation whose descending hemiola continuation grows to great prominence as the climax approaches.[24] Whether one accepts Hahn's description or not, this is one of the most striking of a number of fresh continuations or transformations of the Longing motive that does suggest the possibility of a continuum of meaning in Puffett's sense. The traditional three-part structure of a dance or scherzo can thus be seen in 'Das Tanzlied', though the traditional literal repeat is abandoned for a kind of apotheosis of the Longing theme, which had only a marginal role in the first section.

The concluding B major coda fulfils the characteristics of the epilogue as described by Forchert. The association of B major with this kind of resolution is particularly common in the nineteenth century, notable instances being Tchaikovsky's *Manfred* and *Romeo and Juliet* (before he was prevailed upon to change it by Balakirev), Liszt's Sonata, *Tristan und Isolde* and Delius's setting of *Mitternachtslied Zarathustras* (as he originally entitled the work which was to grow into *A Mass of Life*). The slow epilogue increasingly found a place in Mahler's symphonies as well as providing suitable conclusions for

Ex. 11 bars 737–47

Don Quixote, Ein Heldenleben and *Eine Alpensinfonie*. It was the logical conclusion for an 'autobiographical' symphony, as Mahler's are all too often considered, as well as for Strauss's tone poems in which the 'hero' may be a persona of the composer. What tends to fluctuate in Strauss is the degree of transfiguration present in the closing bars. After *Tod und Verklärung* (and discounting the fairy-tale conclusion of *Till Eulenspiegel*), this element is strongest in *Ein Heldenleben*, in the ending which Strauss grafted on after the work was deemed complete on 1 December 1898.[25] *Also sprach Zarathustra* prefers a rather more attenuated procession into eternity, in keeping with the rather more idealized theme; thus the characteristic string and horn tone gives way to combinations of high woodwind and upper strings. The depths of the orchestra are reserved for Nature and the World Riddle, as if spacing might reinforce the distance between the Superman and the tragic background.

Where formal units are observable in *Zarathustra*, they tend to be the two- and three-part forms described by Waltershausen.[26] The analyst's choice is to posit a grouping based on traditional large-scale form, using sonata and symphonic characteristics as definers of genre and bearers of content, or simply to accept a seemingly value-free series of groupings that points to certain landmarks defined by section headings or musical events. If the latter is the approach, however, then there is seldom any good reason for favouring the two parts of Merian and Wilde, the three of Gerlach, or the four of Del Mar.[27] All of these writers place a sectional division after the great climax at bar 329, all make some use of sonata terminology, and their distinctions seem invariably to fall short of an adequate description because the desire to divide depends on the constant need to discriminate between exposition and development not as sections but as processes. The sectional approach seems a poor substitute for the more frankly rhetorical consideration which springs from Steinitzer, Forchert and Dahlhaus. But the sectional approach has the alternative of variation form to hand, and this has a certain historical plausibility given the use of variations in Strauss's next tone-poem, *Don Quixote*.

Variation, metamorphosis and variant

Unfortunately, the approach that takes variations as starting-point is no less dependent upon cataloguing imprecisions and deviations than those who would like *Zarathustra* to be unequivocally symphonic. Thus Schrenk spoke of 'a kind of variation form', Gysi of the use of variation principles, as though they were only one factor among several.[28] A better attempt to describe the type of variation principle was provided by Muschler, who thought that each section took up the themes of the preceding in a kind of continuous chain of variations that obviously could not be related to the traditional single theme of variation movements.[29] This in his view established the basic formal principle for the rest of Strauss's tone poems. The sections that reflect a kind of variation most clearly are those that fitted the idea of subject groups in the symphonic approach, 'Von den Freuden- und Leidenschaften' and 'Das Grablied'. The manner in which they relate to one another suggests that in a limited sense the variation approach does explain certain features of *Zarathustra*'s processes.

The two sections are not especially close in terms of bars, 'Von den Freuden- und Leidenschaften' containing forty-nine and 'Das Grablied' thirty-seven. This is not necessarily an important factor, however, since Strauss's variation principle in *Don Quixote* is hardly dependent upon the exact proportions of the theme or bass. His approach is that of the character variation, selecting features from his theme for expansion in sections which deviate in greater or lesser degree from the theme. The relationship between the two sections in *Zarathustra* is similar. There are no point-by-point correspondences; motives from the first are woven into a new continuity in the second. Thus the head motive of 'Das Grablied' in the oboe quickly turns upwards to inaugurate a new chromatic descent. The cor anglais attempts to repeat the figure, but transforms the chromatic descent into a reference to bar 131 of 'Von den Freuden- und Leidenschaften', thus bringing two elements of that section into a closer relationship than had earlier been the case; what had been the head motives of two distinct sections now become a single line (Ex. 12). The accompaniment of the opening is also different. Instead of the Life-urge motive which had thrust upward in the bass of 'Von den Freuden- und Leidenschaften', the Longing motive curves upward before it too falls in a lingering descent.

From bar 170, it is this motive's continuation which provides the strongest thread of continuity, as Strauss freely invents a new rising continuation in the solo violin. Material taken from 'Von den Freuden- und Leidenschaften' takes

Ex. 12 bars 168–72

on the role of counterpoint. When the solo violin reaches its peak at the C major of bar 178, the inevitable decline is counterpointed by other declining figures from the earlier section, thus generating the curious sense of an ecstatic dissolution over a pedal which persists until a clear counterpoint of motives is resumed at bar 180. The C major chord is the most unequivocal tonic in the section, B minor appearing initially in second inversion. Not until bar 184 does the original combination return with Longing pushed back into a middle part in a characteristic piling-up of motivic references that slowly drifts into the stasis of a dominant seventh. Whereas 'Von den Freuden- und Leidenschaften' was essentially a melodic paragraph that occasionally drifted into polyphony, 'Das Grablied' slowly reduces a contrapuntal web to homophony.

While the idea of variations undoubtedly helps in clarifying certain characteristics of Zarathustra, the concept of variation form is an over-simplification. Even the rather amorphous term 'symphonic variations', which tends to mean whatever a composer wants it to mean, is too inaccurate to describe form in the tone poem as a whole. How far such use of variation should be distinguished from Lisztian thematic metamorphosis is debatable. If the essence of such metamorphosis is to take a theme and alter certain parameters while retaining the overall shape, thus producing a new version which functions as a kind of character or unit in a process (which is Liszt's *modus operandi* in *Tasso*, *Les Préludes*, *Mazeppa* or the outer movements of the *Faust-Symphonie*), then Strauss's turning of the Passion motive into the trio of the waltz seems close enough to the procedure to deserve the label. Most of the metamorphoses in *Zarathustra* are from the first half of the work into the waltz. Thematic metamorphosis on the whole is not Strauss's normal mode of procedure, since he prefers to work with shorter figures (or leitmotifs), adding to them progressively more elaborate continuations. Admittedly, there are plenty of examples of this kind of writing in Liszt, particularly in those works which exhibit features of the overture. The use of metamorphosis in the waltz of *Zarathustra* therefore may be seen as a special

Ex. 13 retrograde relationship between Dread and Passion motives

case, appropriate to the same kind of pattern discernible in *Tasso*: 'Lamento e trionfo' (which is also present in Mazeppa's ride through tribulation to apotheosis). Metamorphosis and leitmotif, although seemingly so distinct in their respective emphasis on process and denotation, none the less co-exist in the opera house, in the families of related leitmotifs of Wagner's music dramas. It is therefore appropriate enough to view 'Von den Freuden- und Leidenschaften' and 'Das Grablied' as distinct shades of meaning within a process that does not necessarily depend upon variation form.

What should be resisted is the urge to relate Strauss's procedure indiscriminately to Schoenbergian developing variation, a term which in recent years has become something of an analytical omnium gatherum. There has hardly been a composer after Brahms to whom the label has not been applied, usually fairly loosely. Mahler studies have escaped (following the example of Adorno) into a mode of reception (it is hardly technical analysis) that insists on the variant, not the variation, as 'the technical formula for the epic-novelistic factor of the always entirely different but nevertheless identical shapes'.[30] Given the availability of Straussian narratives to accommodate similar motivic ciphers in a state of flux, the temptation to adapt the principle of the variant is strong, stressing individuality, uniqueness and transformation (however hard that might be to describe) over the Schoenbergian insistence on 'a continuous, developmental process'.[31]

The problem with Strauss's procedure is that he retains both methods of working, the transformation of motives in a continuous process (as exhibited by 'Das Grablied') with a variant procedure that is more rooted in Lisztian metamorphosis. The apparent incompatibility is resolved in his application of something resembling developing variation within sections (though rather more primitively employed than in Brahms), and transformed variants of themes as characters over the course of the whole work. There are examples in *Zarathustra* where the categories seem uncertainly to overlap, as in Wilde's demonstration of a retrograde relationship between the Faith and the Passion motives, a connection which is motivic while offering support to Muschler's viewpoint (Ex. 13).[32] Effectively Strauss employs a degree of organization by variation within an associative overview, and if the structural basis of *Zarathustra* is essentially a matter of associations even at the level of keys, forms and thematic material, then at least one conclusion is inescapable. However false the view that *Zarathustra* demonstrates an abstract philosophical argument, there can be no doubt that the various narratives of the previous chapters are as valid a mode of description of the work's procedure as any attempt to describe it in purely musical terms. As Dahlhaus pointed out, the poetic is not a condition of genres (and their characteristics) but of works.[33] Conversely, tone poems hardly constitute a genre in any real sense, but merely exhibit generic characteristics.

8

Rhetoric

Musical rhetoric is a venerable concept, which has been a marked feature of German music theory, partly as a legacy of the Baroque and Classical periods, partly as a result of the preoccupation with *Musiksprache* in more recent times. In English, 'musical language' as applied to individual composers has tended to be more a reflection of what Leonard G. Ratner describes as cohesive musical techniques, rather than the eloquence with which these are employed (thus in agreement with the rather controversial recent tendency to separate analysis and criticism).[1] Yet if such factors as harmony, texture and counterpoint are taken as contributing to a kind of musical expression (which was Strauss's goal, however it be defined), then analysis of techniques and their eloquence as forms of expression (not as what is expressed) are closely interlinked. In this light, doubts about the waltz, for example, are often expressed in terms of musical eloquence, though it is arguable that they have fairly precise equivalents in the sphere of musical organization. This is surprising in that 'Das Tanzlied', by its transforming function and Zarathustrian symbolism, should be the unifying climax of the work, and Strauss's reputation as one of the great masters of the orchestral climax is secure. His timing of the successive waves of musical motion seems self-evident, whether in 'Von der grossen Sehnsucht', 'Das Grablied' or 'Der Genesende'.

In this perhaps resides a clue as to how Strauss's structure should be viewed. To regard *Also sprach Zarathustra* in an architectural sense is less convincing than seeing it as the expression of a dynamic form-concept such as is expressed by Ernst Kurth, whose harmonic approach to form seems to parallel Strauss's use of harmonic relationships as the material from which thematic forms and transformations may be created. In Kurth's study of Romantic harmony, Strauss stands out as a representative figure whose style intensifies Wagner's use of neighbouring notes and chromatic alteration. At the same time, he presages the dissolution of tonality by his dissociation of line from its underlying harmony and by his use of unresolved dissonance.[2] But his personal amalgam of such features with more conventional technical characteristics suggests similar reflections to Lee A. Rothfarb's thoughts on the formal implications of Kurth's theory.

The stress throughout is on motion, from motive to *Bewegungszug*, from absolute chord to extratonal progression. The ebb and flow of psychic motion, once actualized in sound, guarantees continuity. A piece of music, then, is *shaped* psychic motion. The particular shape that motion takes in a work amounts to its musical form.[3]

In *Zarathustra*, the shaping principle, the unresolved opposition of C and B, is a special form of late Romantic tonal expansion. What matters is not their control of this or that block, but the constant overflowing of the tonalities' energies into new cycles or, as Kurth tended to call them, waves of modulatory energy. The harmonic indeterminacy of 'Von der grossen Sehnsucht' in Kurth's system becomes a wave of expansion (which he termed exterior). Its counterpart (so-called interior expansion) is founded on mediant relationships and is also present, if secondary, in *Zarathustra*, between A♭ and B (enharmonically C♭), and in localized progressions between triads, which tend to be elaborations decorating more conventional progressions round the circle of fifths. Oddly enough, A♭ and C are seldom brought into direct contact outside 'Das Tanzlied'. The opposition of C and B may be seen as an attempt to place limits upon the tendency of chromatic harmony to spill over without direction. The formal parallel to this chromatic expansion is the extreme tension between symmetry and asymmetry in phrases, periods and intermediate musical structures.[4] Kurth's implicit relationship between certain types of harmonic motion characteristic of musical Romanticism and forms of organization both of counterpoint and phrase, is a pointer to the manner in which Strauss lays out the successive waves of musical motion in *Zarathustra*, and perhaps forms a more convincing picture of its internal operations and its capacity to generate convincing musical rhetoric than the more architectonic approaches of the previous chapter.

In addition to being the focus of long-range tonal strategy, the opposition of C and B is used frequently as an agent of local tension. The contrast between the two keys is shown at its most drastic in bars 329–40 of 'Der Genesende', where they stand in as incomprehensible an antagonism as in the final bars. Some sections move over their course from one to the other, as in 'Von der grossen Sehnsucht', which starts in B minor but moves to the dominant of C minor; a reverse motion can be seen in the fugue, and in bars 348–408 of 'Der Genesende'. The latter sub-section has a particularly interesting strategy, since the string and woodwind unison that launches it reverses the cycles of fifths from the fugal sections. The line outlines triads of B minor,

E, A, D, G and C majors (bars 348–52), then repeats the process (bars 354–8). In a single line, previous musical arguments seem to be reversed in drastic compression. Sometimes the opposition is the starting-point for a wider harmonic sweep. This is particularly noticeable in the final section of 'Das Tanzlied', which begins with successive eight-bar statements of the Longing theme in C and B majors (bars 685–700). The opposition so bluntly expressed then develops into a large-scale passage through a variety of seventh chords and triads: F, then E♭, G and B (an example of Kurth's interior, third-based expansion), followed by A, before C is restored by a chromatic progression at Figure 44. The contrast between this and the ensuing climax is defined at a technical level by the much stronger sense of orthodox progression which sets in at 44. Whereas tonality is veiled by the chromatic section, the aftermath is emphatically in C major for several pages.

C and B appear to act both as organizing forces and as mutual destabilizers in the harmonic world of *Zarathustra*. Their alternation is dependent upon three basic principles: immediate juxtaposition, cycles of fifths, and chromatic interludes with a high preponderance of unrelated triads and sevenths. Whether analysts should attempt to make a deeper investigation of their relationship depends on how these principles are interpreted. If stylistic factors are taken into account, then the pairing can be seen as a special case of what Willi Schuh takes as 'a hallmark of Strauss's later harmonic style'.[5] His comment refers to the juxtaposition of triads a tritone apart, as in the adjacent triads of E♭ and A in the fugue subject. The relationship of C and B is rather more complex if tritonal oppositions are taken as a defining factor. The tritonal opposite of C is F♯ major, the dominant of B, which in turn is the tritonal opposite of F, the subdominant of C. There are at least three places where Strauss brings elements of this relationship into close contact. In the introduction, the bassoons' F minor (bar 26) is clearly the subdominant of C minor; a few bars later it is replaced by B minor (albeit in second inversion). This progression recurs later in veiled form in bars 159–64 as the link between 'Von den Freuden- und Leidenschaften' and 'Das Grablied'. It is then varied at the great caesura in 'Der Genesende', in keeping with the altered aspect of the introduction at its recall. B minor (bar 338) this time is replaced by F minor after three bars, which then sinks down into a chromatic sequence of diminished sevenths to C major (which in this context feels like the dominant of F minor).

The consequences of such tritonal relationships for Strauss's music have been spelled out most clearly by Graham H. Phipps in a study of *Don Quixote*. This occurs in the context of a discussion of tritone equivalence, an idea derived from Schoenberg's theories of tonal harmony.[6] That a theory of tonal axes resides within Schoenberg's notion of harmonic regions is suggested in *Structural Functions of Harmony*, where the various keys related to C major rest virtually in three horizontal layers in a diagrammatic presentation (simplified here):[7]

```
G♯                          D♭

g♯                          d♭

    E   e   G   g   B♭  b♭

C♯                          G♭

c♯                          g♭

    A   a   C   c   E♭  e♭

F♯                          C♭

f♯                          c♭

    D   d   F   f   A♭  a♭

B                           F♭

b                           f♭
```

Schoenberg is principally interested in the vertical groupings, with the close relative keys G and F clustered round the tonic C, together with their tonic minors; relative minors and majors with further parallel forms spread out in less strong relationships to the truly distant chord forms, a classification which Schoenberg later refines.[8] But there are systems in which three horizontal axes, tonic, dominant and subdominant, are extracted, most notably that of Ernö Lendvai:[9]

```
V:    C♯  E   G   B♭

I:    F♯  A   C   E♭

IV:   B   D   F   A♭
```

In the subdominant axis here, B (and D and A♭) may substitute for F as a kind of subdominant.

In English-speaking analysis, the theories of Lendvai tend to arouse a certain, perhaps forgivable, exasperation. Yet his eccentric formulations frequently have echoes of Schoenberg's more empirically observed theories. Thus the idea that Strauss frequently brings into play the four 'different bass

Ex. 14 The four roots of the diminished seventh and the octatonic scale

tones for a diminished seventh chord', meaning the imaginary roots which Schoenberg's theory employed to explain the diminished seventh (Ex. 14), inevitably generates a pitch collection such as Lendvai uses to generate his 1:2 model (otherwise the octatonic scale).[10] Such demonstrations of theoretical conceits do not 'justify' regarding F and B as a subdominant axis in *Zarathustra*. But of all the keys touched upon in the tone poem, those of such a subdominant axis tend to be more prolonged than others, particularly A♭ in 'Von den Hinterweltlern' and Hahn's 'Nachtlied', B throughout, and F in the limited role defined above. D too has its advocates, notably Murphy, who finds instances of it linked to B, most notably at bars 268–71 and 370–8, though since the latter is represented only by its dominant seventh, the argument is a poor one.[11] A better instance might be the climax on D major at bar 848, where that triad in inversion is the focus for a particularly powerful statement of the Longing theme before C major is restored in preparation for the midnight bell. Few of these statements of F and D would satisfy a really rigorous analyst as to their status as keys. All too often they are chordal events without the deeper structural status that accrues from the presence of their dominants.

Very few tonal areas in *Zarathustra* achieve such a degree of structural importance outside the waltz. It is only in that section that the dominant of C is established as a key in its own right, an event marked by a particularly imposing statement of the hemiola descending figure (bars 584–613). So late an entry of the key on the dominant points to the flimsy role it plays as anything other than a harmonic resource in the first half of the work. In this it is not alone. E♭ is briefly established in 'Von den Freuden- und Leidenschaften' (bars 136–42), but only C, B and A♭ truly establish themselves at any length. Within areas controlled by them, Strauss's repertory of harmonic devices is remarkably constant. Cadence points are often of surprising simplicity, as is the norm in his other works of this period. The complicating factor is usually some form of chromatic side-slip, which is

Ex. 15 *Also sprach Zarathustra*, bars 39–42

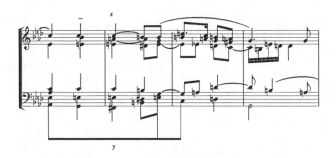

clarified by the subsequent cadence. The second phrase of 'Von den Hinterweltlern' is typical (Ex. 15). After the definition of A♭ in the first phrase, a chromatic descent in the bass leads to the apparently surprising chord of E minor (bar 40). The Wagnerian half-diminished seventh plays a role in this shift as a passing chord (Ex. 15*x*). E minor is a link (enharmonically representing the triad on the flattened submediant F♭) between A♭ and C, the subdominant of G. The bass thus is partitioned into the typical late-nineteenth century pattern of two consecutive major thirds (Ex. 15*y*); to describe this as an interior form of expansion signifies that the cycle will be completed by a return to A♭ (as happens through E major later in the section). When C has been reached in the bass, the cadence into G is of a simplicity that seems slightly sanctimonious, an impression heightened by the presence of the organ.

Much of 'Von den Hinterweltlern' involves such chromatic side-slips. As the tension increases, however, Strauss resorts increasingly to the six-four to achieve the effects of sudden harmonic clarification which are the decisive feature of his style. At first these seem relatively arbitrary. After quitting G, the music drifts back through E♭ major by step-wise motion in the bass, only for an apparently unexpected fall on to a six-four chord of A minor (Ex. 16*x*). The qualifying 'apparently' is necessary, since the diminished seventh that links E♭ to A can be viewed as being close to E♭ as the dominant of the dominant, or to A minor, also as the dominant of the dominant, depending on which of Schoenberg's missing roots is selected to explain the harmony (Ex. 16*y*). Reinterpreting the chord with a different imaginary root (D) enables the next six-four to enter as C minor (Ex. 16*z*). As is Strauss's habit, the progression culminates in two six-fours, of E major – seemingly the climax – then A♭ major. Such gradual intensification (which is paralleled in the

Ex. 16 bars 47–51

increasing density of the string textures) also tends towards clarification, since the climax of the wandering from A♭ is a tonal resource, a dominant seventh on E, which turns out to be the German sixth of A♭, a chord which traditionally demands to be resolved on to the second inversion of the tonic as an approach to a perfect cadence. E and A♭ (enharmonically G♯) thus exhibit that mediant relationship isolated by Kurth. The modernity of Strauss's harmonic style turns out to be founded upon harmonic procedures that were already securely integrated into common practice tonality in Schubert (and indeed earlier). However complex the dissonances and the methods required to analyse them, the resolution is always at this period quite secure, perhaps even, in comparison with what Mahler and Pfitzner were about to do, a little archaic. But this mixture of the archaic and post-Wagnerian chromaticism was itself part of the style of the age, as an examination of Mahler's settings of *Des Knaben Wunderhorn* or Pfitzner's String Quartet in D major reveals.

In the more developmental sections of the score, Strauss's harmonic resources are usually much freer. Thus the rather improvisatory passage in 'Von der grossen Sehnsucht' (bars 81–99) proceeds mostly by step-wise voice-leading, avoiding clearly expressed tonics (Ex. 17). The suggestion of C major often cited as bitonal (bar 82) is a fairly exact foreshadowing of the conclusion (see Ex. 7a on page 71), a French sixth constructed over the Phrygian second, to which the purely motivic G adds a certain mild irregularity. Precisely the same effect is used at bar 263 in 'Von der Wissenschaft', though there the tension escapes into F major. Here the passage drifts to a six-four of D major,

Ex. 17 bars 81–99, harmonic outline

Mag – ni – fi – cat

with a suspended G to accommodate the Gregorian fragment of the *Magnificat*. Thereupon the chromatic voice-leading highlights a six-four of G minor before a diminished seventh leads to a six-four of C minor, the key of 'Von den Freuden- und Leidenschaften'. Strauss maintains a 'developmental' tension by refusing to move unequivocally to any key. Even after reaching the C minor six-four, there is a further chromatic extension which delays the release on to the dominant of C minor. In such passages, Strauss conforms to the notion of 'flexible, fluctuating' tonality such as Schoenberg defined, perhaps also to that 'suspended tonality' in which 'Every major or minor triad could be interpreted as a key, even if only in passing'.[12]

The theoretical interpretation of Strauss's predilection for the six-four involves certain general principles for analysing his music; the question of whether Strauss viewed the six-four as basically a suspension (i.e., a contrapuntal event) or as a chord inversion (a harmonic event) cannot be given a simple answer from *Zarathustra*, where both interpretations seem to be implied. It is clearly resolved on to a five-three in such cases as bars 153–7. In 'Das Grablied', the chords D–F♯–B and F♯–B–D do duty for the missing statement of the root-position triad of B minor, though in many such cases it is possible to imagine the resolution on to a five-three (F♯–A♯–C♯) as postponed until a much later stage (or a higher structural level), such as the close of the section. This also is a possible interpretation of the harmonic structure of 'Nachtwandlerlied', which begins its protracted cadencing in B over F♯. Whether Strauss regarded the six-four as a suspension over the

Ex. 18 bars 158–9 (bass and harmony only)

dominant or as an inverted tonic is unclear, as it can be in many of the theoretical systems that formed the staple of contemporary music theory.[13]

For the analyst, however, the question is a microcosm of the difficulty in classifying some of Strauss's most characteristic progressions. The chord *x* in Ex. 18a is a case in point. In the celebrated text-book written by Strauss's friend Thuille in collaboration with the Munich critic Rudolf Louis (which may have played a part in shaping Kurth's harmonic theory), this chord must be viewed as chord VII of C minor with a diminished seventh.[14] The fifth is flattened to F♭, and the resulting chord is 'understood as the subdominant', though the E, the enharmonic equivalent of F♭, has been substituted for the subdominant scale-degree F (Ex. 18b).[15] Chord VII comes close in this interpretation to being a tritonal equivalent of the subdominant. In bar 160 a similar phenomenon, enharmonically altered, is read on the other hand as a real E natural, anticipating C in the next bar as a 'leaping changing-note'. Louis and Thuille believed that with this argument they had demonstrated the 'quite simple' basis of 'this only apparently complicated spot'. To one not schooled in their system, the simplicity may seem less evident, and reflects the difficulties that Strauss's harmonies presented to his contemporaries. The problem was not to understand when he was using the standard chromatic resources, but how they should be adapted to theories of harmonic functions. Thus a few bars later (Ex. 19), the chord F–G♯–B–D♯ which ushers in the six-four of B minor required explanation as chord II (F–A♭–C♭–E♭) with a subdominant function in E♭ minor (though why this was necessary here is not clear, given that E♭ minor is not really relevant to this particular motion from C minor to B minor); then as a raised subdominant in B (E♯–G♯–B–D♯). The complexity is appropriate, given the identity of this collection of pitches with

Ex. 19 bars 162–4 (simplified)

Wagner's 'Tristan chord', which similarly defied theorists of harmonic functions.

Nonetheless, Louis and Thuille were grappling with a very real phenomenon, Strauss's use of ambiguous chords of apparently simple formation but with the goal of generating conflict through their context. The modernity in Strauss's style was his capacity to insinuate 'foreign' resources into tonal areas, in the first instance a dominant seventh formation over E♮ in the key of C minor. Quite frequently such irregularities were by-products of themes, a characteristic on which Schoenberg later laid much stress in his discussion of suspended tonality:

> . . . the theme is undoubtedly the crux of the matter. It must give opportunity for such harmonic looseness through its characteristic figurations.[16]

It is the particular feature of the above progression (Ex. 18a) that it is complicated by the Disgust motive in the bass, whose underlying harmonies at its first statement use both Strauss's characteristic chains of diminished sevenths and the Neapolitan sixth (Ex. 20). Although the characteristic tritone of the Disgust motive can be understood within C minor as leading-note and

Ex. 20 bars 150–3 (Disgust and harmonies only)

N6

Ex. 21 bars 265–8

seventh over the dominant, it also enables the motive to adjust to passages of suspended or roving tonality with a degree of comfort. Thus it is not surprising that Strauss should have attempted at one stage to work it into 'Von der grossen Sehnsucht'.[17]

In 'Von der Wissenschaft', the Disgust motive functions regularly as an irritant precisely because the relationship between its initial tritone (F–B) and its concluding augmented triad (E–G♯–C) is capable of multiple interpretation; thus what may decorate the tonic of F major is brought into close conjunction with triads of A and F minor (bars 265–7), facilitating a move to the dominant seventh of G (Ex. 21); the peculiarities of the motive seem for a brief space to dictate the harmonic events. The two ideas, the tritone (with its basis in a cycle of minor thirds) and the augmented triad (with its basis in a cycle of major thirds), are brought into immediate juxtaposition in the sudden violent outburst that precedes 'Der Genesende', where the descending thirds of the violin line contains diminished seventh (x) and augmented triad (y) as well

Ex. 22 bars 278–80

Ex. 23 bars 386 and 400

as the seventh chord (z) that the orchestra has just sounded (Ex. 22). Strauss treats the conflicting outlines in the Disgust motive as an opportunity for generating irregular melodic and contrapuntal events that accordingly disrupt normal tonal expectations.

Other themes are no less able to function ambiguously. With the Disgust motive, the shape of the theme itself was an important factor in suggesting harmonic disruption. In the case of the motive associated with Zarathustra, the disruption is imposed from without by the conflict of B and C. Thus in the retransition section (bars 362–408), Strauss's approach is essentially homophonic, using augmented triads and seventh chords in another passage of suspended tonality. As in Schoenberg's definition, any triad upon which the progression alights is a potential tonic, as with B at bar 381. Zarathustra's theme is heard in this tonal setting as a fundamentally diatonic idea, but is then reinterpreted as the dominant of C with the fifth raised to generate an augmented triad (to which an F is added to create the sonority characteristic of the French sixth). The same theme is thus interpreted to fit both B and C, depending on the long-term shift of F♯ to G in the bass (Ex. 23); that which is diatonic with chromatic neighbouring notes briefly acquires the flavour of the whole-tone scale (also with chromatic neighbouring notes). This augmented sonority becomes the hinge of the retransition, which returns from B to C for 'Das Tanzlied'. In this passage, the themes seem to be adjusted to a definite tonal strategy, whereas the Disgust motive seems to carry alternative tonal strategies within its melodic shape. Two types of contrapuntal writing thus ensue. The older kind is that associated with Wagner, in which a contrapuntal web is an expansion of harmonic progressions into a melodic space. The second type is that which has also been discerned in Mahler and Pfitzner, a counterpoint in which motivic and melodic factors lend coherence to harmonies that lack strong functional direction.

As a result of this fundamental differentiation in his approach to polyphony, Strauss treats the orchestra in a comparably differentiated way. It is arguable that he employs three different methods of organizing polyphonic texture if the fugue of 'Von der Wissenschaft' is taken into account. Here, the polyphonic voice is equated with a specific orchestral sonority, which retains that voice for an extended period, if not for the complete duration of the fugue. Thus in the exposition there may be said to be four string voices, formed by dividing the cellos and basses into four groups, each of which is a polyphonic voice. There is a limit to the applicability of this principle, because Strauss compromises it with a further idea, that the fugue should gradually rise through the orchestra as it also rises through the circle of fifths. The pastiche of traditional fugue thus gradually turns into a freer texture, which remains fugal, but adapts to the expressive resources of the nineteenth-century orchestra. Such fugatos which involve a gradual process of textural expansion are known in many earlier composers, as in the finale of the *Symphonie fantastique*; the pattern of strings first, then woodwind is also to be found in numerous other examples of fugal writing (e.g., Liszt's *Prometheus*, and the fugue in 'Purgatorio' from the *Dante Symphony*). Texturally, this fugue is as much of a homage to tradition as in its figuration.

If this is an exception, then other polyphonic textures testify to the position that Strauss occupied at the head of the modernists. One species of orchestral texture may be taken as a liquefaction of the monumental orchestral blocks of the opening. Four- and five-part textures form the basis of most of the self-enclosed sections, such as 'Von den Hinterweltlern', where the organ presents in simplified form the four-part substratum of the increasingly expanded string section. Strauss's principal method of differentiation is to vary the subdivision of the strings, a procedure at which he acquired considerable virtuosity, culminating many years later in *Metamorphosen*. The contrast of single desks at the outset with gradual reinforcement towards the climax is enhanced by the touches of pseudo-polyphony which Strauss adds from bar 52 onwards. The hymnal textures gradually take on the illusion of independent lines, an illusion which quickly lapses as they drift into arpeggios.

Such textures may eventually acquire a more substantial polyphonic content. The climax at bar 585 is witness to this. The main figure, the descending hemiola, is treated imitatively between the outer sections, while the harmonic support acquires an upward-thrusting arpeggio in horns. The harps act as a reminder of the slow progression that underlies the appearance of contrapuntal activity. The texture remains fundamentally homophonic, and this remains true even when Strauss uses the favourite nineteenth-century trick of combining themes in the manner that Berlioz sometimes advertised in his own scores. Thus the A♭ metamorphosis of the Passion theme in 'Das Tanzlied' is stated in its entirety (bars 629–42), succeeded by the gliding motion of the waltz, which is a further metamorphosis from bar 135 of 'Von den Freuden- und Leidenschaften', and then the two ideas are combined at bars 668–9, though Strauss shapes the two together with a feeling for sensuous blend that is quite different from the vivid primary colours that Berlioz, Verdi or Bruckner were likely to use. That the descending violin figure decorates the Passion theme (and not *vice versa*) is shown by the various melodic adjustments that are made to it.

The feeling of a textural kaleidoscope is enhanced by a canonic pre-sentation of the Passion theme. That the two canonic voices are presented in blending timbres (some first violins and horns with lower woodwind and violas lead, followed by solo horn and second violins with some cellos) draws attention to the skill with which Strauss subdivides his large orchestra. That the six horns are present for volume in places is undeniable. But equally they are present for such subdivisions. The whole vision floats over the slow-moving harmonies of trombones and horns (coloured at a much higher octave by flutes) and the even slower motion of the bass. The distinctive Straussian feature is that the swooning decorative descent in all desks of first violins save one attracts the glamour of sonority more fitting to the theme than to the decoration; orchestral foreground and background are interchangeable. Perhaps this is why Strauss's textures here and at bar 178 seem so redolent of the period of *Jugendstil* and *Art Nouveau*. The various sonorous planes create a surface sheen which seems to consume the thematic content.

Set against this enhanced homophony, which is undoubtedly what Strauss's detractors were thinking of when they spoke of him as an 'interior decorator' or 'stage designer', is a more fragmented style of orchestral polyphony. Admittedly *Zarathustra* is not quite so rich in this as later works such as *Ein Heldenleben*, with its carping critics and ferocious battle scene. It is also arguable that both Mahler and Pfitzner were to carry this type of texture to greater lengths, the one in his middle-period instrumental symphonies, the other in the underground caverns of *Die Rose vom Liebesgarten* (though both *Salome* and *Elektra* also represent similar steps on the road to a more radical independent orchestral polyphony). Nonetheless, 'Der Genesende' demonstrates the potential of orchestral textures based on motivic factors with minimal support from sustaining inner parts, particularly from bar 287 to bar 304.

Such orchestral textures are quite different in their modernity from those that are celebrated as 'effect', the evocations of laughter, which impress by their discarding of deep bass (as in bars 251–62). In the retransition, another 'laughing interlude', Strauss combines high texture with subdivision to create a particularly light-footed impression worthy of Zarathustra's characterization as the spirit of 'laughing malice'. But these once notorious examples of 'illustration' are really surprising variants on homophony rather than extensions of polyphony. Inseparable from their originality are the new demands made upon the performers, symbolized by the trumpet's octave leaps, which are seldom performed even by virtuoso players without a fractional but audible readjustment of embouchure from c^2 to c^3. The contrast in orchestral style between homophony and more radical polyphony roughly follows the dividing line between tonally self-contained sections and passages of roving or suspended tonality, but it is in the latter sections that illustrative orchestral writing is also most likely to occur. Both original contrapuntal combinations and startling new textures seem to have been necessary to Strauss to sustain interest in passages where he was most self-consciously 'developing'. Where his thematic 'characters' were in a state of transition, then his virtuosity as an orchestrator served to enhance his ability to prolong harmonic tension. But the control of harmonic tension was still the *sine qua non* of his style.

Periodicity inevitably reflects the distinction between closed forms and open, roving tonality. In addition to the song-like sections, the waltz tends to be organized on quadratic principles. Even the prolonged upbeat to the section (bars 409–28) is a multiple of four bars, though this extended fantasy on the Nature motive conceals exact points of division into four-bar groups. The first two waltz phrases are more clearly four bars each. With the entry of the solo violin's salon melody at bar 441, the four-square nature of the theme construction is underlined by the group of four silent bars which separates the first two phrases. Thereafter Strauss carefully works to convey an impression of irregularity within the predominant grouping:

bars 441–4	4 bars	first phrase	C: I
445–8	4	accompaniment only	
449–52	4	second phrase	
453–4	2	accompaniment only	
455–6	2	two bar upbeat to	
457–60	4	third phrase	V
461–4	4	fourth phrase	V
465–8	4	final tonic	I

The reduction of the accompanimental interlude from a four-bar to a two-bar grouping renders the subsequent phrases more irregular; whether the resolution of bar 465 is an extension of the previous phrase, or a periodic unit in its own right is impossible to determine, particularly since Strauss's phrase markings seem to contradict the four-bar groupings. It presages a new phase, coinciding with a move to A minor and major, in which eight-bar units predominate initially.

However ecstatic the waltz becomes, the underlying structure uses units of two, four or eight bars. The harmonic pattern is no less conventional, with A and E giving way to D by a chromatic side-slip (bar 486) as preparation for the dominant of C. Here Strauss re-emphasizes Zarathustra's theme on the augmented triad as a prelude to a restatement of the opening of the waltz theme; to underscore the sonority, groups of violins scurry downwards in parallel augmented triads (bars 505–19). Such piquant touches, no more than the occasional overlap in the phrase structure, cannot quite conceal the conventionality of Strauss's waltz. Although the traditional Viennese off-beat pattern is not present in its classic form, the arpeggiated patterns in harp and pizzicato strings are fully in keeping with its spirit. The solo violin's thirds and sixths sing of the salon and the ball-room. Gradually the accompaniment generates irregularities: the first violins play cross-string arpeggios in duple time, semiquaver upbeats curl round the bars of the dance, but scoops to high harmonics persistently remind us of that side of Strauss who wanted to emulate his famous Viennese namesakes. Later a greater momentum begins to set in, partly the product of hemiola, partly the result of Strauss's wide-ranging chromatic excursions, which threaten to engulf the Viennese trappings in a form of motivic development alien to the extended melodies of the genre. With this, the rather lush simplicity of Strauss's waltz begins to acquire a much more shameless vulgarity, which only achieves its apotheosis after the interlude in A♭.

In such music, symbol seems almost more important than material. Ask the music not what it is, but what it stands for, Strauss seems to say. For much of this period in music history, the waltz did carry the same sort of charge that the scherzo had for Beethoven, an expression of some form of elemental energy such as coursed through the great dance cycles of the younger Johann Strauss. Admittedly it also had a comfortable bourgeois side: not only in *Der Rosenkavalier*, but in Zemlinsky's *Kleider machen Leute*, did the waltz stand for a certain type of contentment, a domestic complaisance allied to the easily manufactured excitement of the salon that fitted both Faninal's (rather than the Marschallin's) Vienna and Gottfried Keller's Goldach in Zemlinsky's opera. But there was also an apocalyptic aspect to the waltz, present in Mahler, burlesqued by Ravel, and seized upon by Strauss for such quite different dances as those of Zarathustra, Salome or Elektra.

Describing the waltz-like scherzo of his Fifth Symphony, Mahler spoke of 'a comet's tail', 'the expression of incredible energy' and 'a human being in the full light of day, in the prime of his life'.[18] He did not succeed in finding this quality so readily in Strauss's waltzes, judging by his opinion of Salome's dance, but his comments accurately catch the almost cosmic energy that composers attempted to unleash. The Viennese waltz became a symbol for a society without constraint that is laughable as a description of its Viennese origins, but seemed suitable to Strauss for Nietzsche's superhuman laughter. Its pattern is thus waltz, contrast, apocalypse, the salon gradually being swallowed in both the darkness of the Nietzschean midnight, and the light of the Eternal Recurrence. Of his scherzo, Mahler noted that the nocturnal harp and cor anglais would be excluded, and he was almost as good as his word (apart from the cor anglais in bars 224–85). Strauss on the other hand allotted these symbolic instruments a central place in his dance, as witness of its double aspect.

Strauss's critics were quick to notice that he had copied his model a little too well in the waltz. To accommodate Zarathustra's dancing humour required an energy that was not latent in the solo violin's melody. It is hardly surprising that Strauss threw it over for transformations of earlier material. In the final apocalypse, however, quadratic phrasing sometimes sits uneasily beside the transformation and fragmentation of thematic material. The thread of continuity is broken, existing neither in the motivic events nor in the regular succession of bar groups. From bar 805, the succession of Zarathustra's theme, Disgust, Faith and the middle section of the Passion motive, each of four bars, seems to be dictated by the idea that there should be a transfiguration of themes; the transfiguration is not demonstrated 'eloquently', however, since the fragments remain obstinately discrete in their lack of cohesion. The pulse of the music momentarily flags; musical ideas seem tied to a pre-existing harmonic scheme which dictates a large detour round the chromatic spectrum before the final climax chords. It is a relief when the powerful statement of Longing on a first inversion of D plunges the music into its all-engulfing C major. In truth, Strauss saw the symbolic vulgarity of the waltz and tried to break its bounds, but the homophonic nature of the waltz was never quite jettisoned for the kind of contrapuntal energy that makes Mahler's scherzo rather more daemonic in its effect. One remains too conscious of the genre with Strauss, to the detriment of the expressive goal. This criticism is not at all the same as the view that the waltz is a vulgar blot on the work. To the contrary, it is most vital where it is most vulgar, least convincing when it attempts to unite this vulgarity with symphonic pretensions.

The technical aspect of the waltz that critics most deplored was a special case of a generally perceived weakness, thematic invention. This has rhythmical and melodic aspects which sometimes proceed from genre. Thus the choice of the waltz for 'Das Tanzlied', with its specific generic associations, more or less dictated the character of the invention: four-square, stressed second beats, hemiolas, and a conventional type of conjunct motion with small leaps. Something of the same conventionality was more or less prescribed for the hymnal melody of 'Von den Hinterweltlern'. Strauss's individuality in such cases was the manipulation of the melody in order to reveal a greater compass lurking within the conventional. His love of high violins is of a piece with his later glorification of the soprano voice, the high compass in which the initially baritonal nature of much of his invention found its final expressive release. Such melodic proliferation may be seen as the specifically Straussian form of what Ratner terms simple melody.[19]

A complex, figural type of melody is generated from the evolution of the motive. Thus the Longing theme consists of an arpeggiated *Urmotif*, but gradually expands its tailpiece to the point where, in 'Nachtwandlerlied', the continuation becomes the melody. Complex figural melody eventually turns into pure *cantilena*, symbolized by the relegation of the *Urmotif* to a contrapuntal part (Ex. 24). But the need to integrate motives into line is still demonstrated by the use of Disgust within the seemingly pure diatonicism of the *cantilena* (bars 960–4). It helps to intensify the musical direction, enabling Strauss to break out of the underlying alternation of six-four and five-three. Thirds with chordal accompaniment gradually turn into chromaticism, which prepares the elegiac interpolation of the subdominant between dominant and final tonic (bar 965).

Ex. 24 bars 953–7

Even in Strauss's vision of eternity, there is thus a balance between *cantilena*, a category with its roots in simple rhythms and conjunct motion with small leaps, and the disruptive force of the motive; for the one, diatonic means and periodicity are sufficient, for the other, chromaticism and the disturbing of the symmetry of phrasing. This type of balance between closed forms and disruptive forces is more or less constant for Strauss's style. It is present in *Salome* and *Elektra*, which tilt the balance towards the motive and disruption, and in *Der Rosenkavalier* and *Ariadne auf Naxos*, which favour the *cantilena* and symmetry. But no work before the final period exclusively favours one over the other. *Also sprach Zarathustra* employs them as one form of opposition in much the same spirit as C and B, but whereas they constitute the barriers for a historical tonal expansion, *cantilena* and motive, periodicity and asymmetry represent Strauss's personal definition of the limits of a late Romantic music. They may also be said to represent different visions of the characters or shapes with which he sought to replace Lisztian development: in place of complex developments, categories of invention expressive in themselves. That, rather than profoundly new types of melodic invention such as Wagner pioneered, was Strauss's originality.

9

Afterword

A footnote of interest to any study of *Also sprach Zarathustra* is the degree to which the influence of Nietzsche continued to affect Strauss. His comments upon Nietzsche remain tantalizing, though at least one clear point emerges. Strauss remained uneasy about Nietzsche's views on the history of music and on Wagner's place within it. A comment in a letter to Wolfgang Golther of 5 April 1945 sets Nietzsche entirely in a musical perspective:

How many men know what German music is? At any rate not the philosophical gentlemen! Schopenhauer stopped already at Rossini, and a naive string quartet by Dittersdorf was the summit of music for the good Oswald Spengler. The puffed-up philosopher Nietzsche perhaps had a mild suspicion, but not more, though he remained dependent at least on the splendid *Carmen*![1]

A year later, another letter stressed the 'aesthetic enjoyment' of Nietzsche's *Zarathustra*, though otherwise he had little good to say, even employing the familiar image of the 'sick' philosopher to denigrate the significance of his achievement.[2]

Strauss seems to have returned in old age to his earlier picture of Nietzsche: brilliant insights in the midst of much that was wrong-headed, particularly about Wagner and music. Earlier, he had more positive thoughts, which are still consistent with this general trend. In a letter to Hofmannsthal of 1 June 1925, he was prepared to admit that Nietzsche might be one of a select few (others being more emphatically Goethe, Schiller and Wagner) with whom one could 'discuss the nature of artistic creation'.[3] He had just been re-reading *Die Geburt der Tragödie* 'with tremendous relish!'; that it should have been the book by Nietzsche most under the thrall of Wagner's influence is an obvious pointer to the way in which he later came to read Nietzsche. Appropriately, the most Nietzschean of his later works, *Daphne*, features Apollonian and Dionysian elements which are most characteristic of *Die Geburt der Tragödie*.[4]

There remains one strong piece of evidence of the full impact of Nietzsche on Strauss, and that is the linking of *Eine Alpensinfonie* to Nietzsche's late book

Der Antichrist (1888), a subject that was raised surprisingly by Del Mar, who, though having no apparent access to the sketchbooks for the work, still felt that there was an affinity between *Also sprach Zarathustra* and the 'Alpine' Symphony which resided in 'the supernatural, even the transcendental, in a way which is hauntingly beautiful and vivid'; these qualities were also to be discerned, interestingly, in *Die Frau ohne Schatten*.[5] Del Mar thus selected three of the most controversial works by Strauss, objects of suspicion to many critics but of near idolatry to many Straussians, as representing some quality that was otherwise unusual in the composer.

Subsequently, the sketchbooks of *Eine Alpensinfonie* substantially revealed the extent to which Strauss had contemplated linking the subject to another Nietzschean scenario. Once more nature, sunrise, mountains and an ascent (apparently all too physical) stand in a Nietzschean perspective.[6] Strauss seems again in his comments to set the naivety of religion in contrast with individual self-responsibility; the might of nature is set against the religious sentiments of childhood, the growth of individual thought is stressed, and a strange succession of images seems to consign religion to the sleep of reason: 'Träume u. Gespenster (nach Goya)' ('Dreams and ghosts (after Goya)') and 'Dämonen u. Gespenster: ein Autodafé'. The Nietzschean idea seems strongest in the earliest stages of what was a long process of gestation (1902–13). The 'Goya' annotations are quite persistent for a time, but seem to belong to a phase when the work was considered as a four-movement symphony rather than its final single-movement form. At one stage beauty is defined as 'Harmonie im Schaffen', which seems to connect with *Ein Heldenleben* and 'The Hero's works of peace' rather than *Zarathustra*. Nature has a rather different emphasis here than it has in *Zarathustra*, with the intended final movement at one stage being envisaged as 'Befreiung in der Natur' ('liberation into nature'); this seems to correspond to an earlier idea, the beginnings of independent thought, which was then reshaped to 'Befreiung durch *die Arbeit*' ('liberation through work'). Nature, independent thought and creation seem to be linked here in Strauss's mind; nature is no longer a riddle to be solved. The title, *Der Antichrist*, from Nietzsche's most sustained onslaught on Christianity, its founder and its values, seems to be a symbol of the forces that inhibit the individual.

As the work evolved, the annotations came more and more to concentrate on the physical aspects, mountains, waterfall, glacier, storm and the climb. That the climber had the Wagnerian-Nietzschean description, 'Der Wanderer', begins to recede in importance. In 1902, 'the wanderer is almost buried beneath the rock-slides'; in 1913, 'rock falls begin to roll down under the water'. But *Der Antichrist* is still retained as a title in the latest stages, and the published score still retains the section heading 'Vision' amidst the matter-of-fact references to storms and glaciers. A symbolical core of meaning is still present. Nietzsche retained the capacity to urge Strauss to create, even if he finally withheld the initial spark from his audience. In this may perhaps be seen a final reaction to the critical onslaught upon the 'abstraction' underlying *Zarathustra*; superficially Nietzsche's *Antichrist* operates at a greater level of abstraction than *Also sprach Zarathustra*. Strauss permitted the trappings of illustrative, programmatic music to go forward, but withheld the deeper implications of his work from a public which he could not trust to understand his intentions. Nowadays *Eine Alpensinfonie*, like *Zarathustra*, is a showpiece for virtuoso orchestras in digital sound.

Notes

1 'Freely after Nietzsche'

1 Max Steinitzer, *Richard Strauss*, p. 60; see also John Williamson, 'Strauss and *Macbeth*', pp. 3–21.
2 Franz Trenner (ed.), *Cosima Wagner-Richard Strauss: Ein Briefwechsel*, p. 222.
3 Hans Merian, *Richard Strauss' Tondichtung 'Also sprach Zarathustra'*, pp. 16–21.
4 Hermann W. von Waltershausen, *Richard Strauss: Ein Versuch*, p. 66.
5 Ernest Newman, *Richard Strauss*, pp. 76–7; Karl Schmalz, 'Richard Strauss' *Also sprach Zarathustra* und *Ein Heldenleben*', p. 102.
6 Norman Del Mar, *Richard Strauss: A Critical Commentary*, vol. 1, p. 132.
7 Leopold Schmidt, *Aus dem Musikleben der Gegenwart*, p. 275; Waltershausen, *Richard Strauss: Ein Versuch*, p. 65. There is a germ of interest here, in that *Zarathustra* is linked in several rather tangential ways to Strauss's operatic plans. Its programme touches upon a famous controversy about Strauss's first opera, *Guntram*; its sketches overlap with those for an intended opera on Goethe's *Lila* and Ernst von Wolzogen was moved to propose the collaboration that produced *Feuersnot* (the second of Strauss's operas) by a performance of *Zarathustra* (Franz Grasberger and Franz Hadamowsky (eds.), *Richard-Strauss-Ausstellung zum 100. Geburtstag*, p. 70).
8 Carl Dahlhaus, *Nineteenth-Century Music*, pp. 360–1.
9 Richard Strauss, *Betrachtungen und Erinnerungen*, p. 211.
10 *Ibid.*, p. 210.
11 Carl Dahlhaus, *Klassische und romantische Musikästhetik*, pp. 386–8.

2 The Straussian tone poem as drama

1 Steinitzer, *Richard Strauss*, p. 46.
2 Friedrich von Hausegger, *Die Musik als Ausdruck*, p. 121.
3 Hans Heinrich Eggebrecht, 'Symphonische Dichtung', pp. 223–6; Dahlhaus, *Klassische und romantische Musikästhetik*, p. 389.
4 Eggebrecht, 'Symphonische Dichtung', p. 230.
5 Hugo Botstiber, *Geschichte der Ouvertüre*, p. 215.
6 Friedrich von Hausegger, *Gedanken eines Schauenden*, p. 258.
7 Eggebrecht, 'Symphonische Dichtung', p. 228.
8 Sander L. Gilman (ed.), *Conversations with Nietzsche: A Life in the Words of His Contemporaries*, trans. David J. Parent (New York/Oxford: OUP, 1987), p. 142.
9 There is something a little unbelievable about Romain Rolland's claim that Strauss thought the character of Zarathustra an invention of Nietzsche. Rolland's whole attitude to Strauss suggests a certain unwillingness to regard him as his intellectual equal; see Rollo Myers (ed.), *Richard Strauss and Romain Rolland*, p. 134.
10 Strauss, *Betrachtungen und Erinnerungen*, pp. 11–13; see also Alfred Lorenz, 'Der formale Schwung in Richard Strauss' *Till Eulenspiegel*', p. 658.
11 Although often presented as a conservative figure by Straussians (including Strauss himself in later years), Thuille for a time was just as susceptible to Ritter's influence: see Willi Schuh,

Richard Strauss, pp. 35–6, and Friedrich Munter, *Ludwig Thuille. Ein erster Versuch* (Munich: Drei Masken, 1923), pp. 20, 26–8.

12 Alan Walker, *Franz Liszt*, vol. 2, *The Weimar Years 1848–1861* (London: Faber, 1989), p. 197.

13 Siegmund von Hausegger, *Alexander Ritter: Ein Bild seines Charakters und Schaffens* (Berlin: Marquardt, 1907), pp. 120–2.

14 Gerald Abraham (ed.), *The New Oxford History of Music*, vol. 9, *Romanticism 1830–1890* (Oxford: OUP, 1990), pp. 510–11.

15 Willi Schuh and Franz Trenner (eds.), *Hans von Bülow and Richard Strauss: Correspondence*, p. 81–3.

16 Franz Trenner (ed.), *Richard Strauss-Ludwig Thuille: Ein Briefwechsel*, pp. 115–16.

17 R. W. S. Mendl, 'The art of the symphonic poem', pp. 451–2. The idea of the musical instrument as medium for an emotional 'language' can also be seen in Friedrich von Hausegger's appraisal of Liszt the pianist; see *Gedanken eines Schauenden*, pp. 249–51.

18 Franz Trenner, *Die Skizzenbücher von Richard Strauss*, p. 4; the translation follows the excellent one by Mary Whittall in Schuh, *Richard Strauss*, p. 421. It is divided rather differently in accordance with its lay-out on Strauss's page, to which Whittall presumably did not have access. I have also substituted 'character' for 'form' on each occasion as a translation of *Gestalt*. This seems more consistent with the talk of a 'purely human drama'; 'form' on the other hand may be more appropriate to the reference to absolute music. Either way, the passage seems to lose a dimension of meaning in translation.

19 'On Franz Liszt's symphonic poems', in *Richard Wagner's Prose Works* (8 vols., London, 1898), vol.3, pp. 235–54; Dahlhaus, *Klassische und romantische Musikästhetik*, pp. 414–28 (the specific essay in this collection, 'Wagner und die Programmusik', is translated by Paul A. Mackenzie (et al.) in *Studies in Romanticism*, 9 (1970), pp. 3–20).

20 'On the overture', in *Richard Wagner's Prose Works*, vol. 7, p. 159.

21 'On the application of music to drama', in *Richard Wagner's Prose Works*, vol. 6, p. 179.

22 'On Franz Liszt's symphonic poems', pp. 249–50.

23 Dahlhaus, *Klassische und romantische Musikästhetik*, p. 424.

24 'On Franz Liszt's symphonic poems', p. 251.

3 Strauss's individualism

1 *Wagner-Strauss Briefwechsel*, p. 155.

2 Schuh, *Richard Strauss*, pp. 283–8; *Strauss-Thuille Briefwechsel*, pp. 127–9.

3 *Wagner-Strauss Briefwechsel*, p. 155.

4 Willi Schuh (ed.), *Richard Strauss: Briefe an die Eltern 1882–1906*, p. 173.

5 Schuh, *Richard Strauss*, p. 294; Roswitha Schlötterer, 'Richard Strauss und sein Münchner Kreis', p. 18.

6 Seidl's essay is reprinted in his *Straussiana: Aufsätze zur Richard-Strauss-Frage aus drei Jahrzehnten*; see also Seidl, *Moderner Geist in der deutschen Tonkunst*, p. 87, and Richard Batka, *Richard Strauss*, p. 9.

7 Seidl, *Straussiana*, pp. 33 and 44; Batka, *Richard Strauss*, p. 9. Stirner's doctrine, 'die Selbstherrlichkeit des Individuums', was frequently used as a political slogan at the turn of the century: see R. Hinton Thomas, *Nietzsche in German Politics and Society 1890–1918* (Manchester: Manchester University Press, 1983), p. 31.

8 See Roswitha Schlötterer (ed.), *Richard Strauss-Max von Schillings: Ein Briefwechsel*, pp. 44–5.

9 *Strauss: Briefe an die Eltern*, pp. 160–2.

10 Seth Taylor, *Left-Wing Nietzscheans: The Politics of German Expressionism 1910–1920* (Berlin/New York: de Gruyter, 1990), pp. 145–6.

11 For Nietzsche and Stirner, see George Woodcock, *Anarchism* (rev. edn, Harmondsworth: Pelican, 1975), p. 88; see also John Henry Mackay, *Max Stirner: Sein Leben und sein Werk* (2nd

edn, Treptow: Bernhard Zack, 1910), pp. 10 and 21. Bülow's enthusiasm stemmed from personal knowledge of Stirner, and is comparable with his interest in Ferdinand Lassalle.

12 Trenner, *Die Skizzenbücher von Richard Strauss*, p. 6.

13 Gary Shapiro, *Nietzschean Narratives* (Bloomington: Indiana University Press, 1989), p. 92.

14 Leslie Paul Thiele, *Friedrich Nietzsche and the Politics of the Soul: A Study of Heroic Individualism* (Princeton: Princeton University Press, 1990), p. 45.

15 For the creator as destroyer, see Laurence Lampert, *Nietzsche's Teaching*, pp. 62–3.

16 For the creative individual and revaluation, see Bruce Detwiler, *Nietzsche and the Politics of Aristocratic Radicalism* (Chicago: University of Chicago, 1990), p. 105.

17 See Lampert, *Nietzsche's Teaching*, pp. 62–3; Thiele, *Nietzsche and the Politics of the Soul*, p. 45.

18 See also Thiele, *Nietzsche and the Politics of the Soul*, p. 44.

19 Detwiler, *Nietzsche and the Politics of Aristocratic Radicalism*, p. 105; Mark Warren, *Nietzsche and Political Thought* (Cambridge, Mass.: MIT, 1988), pp. 178 and 240.

20 Warren, *Nietzsche and Political Thought*, p. 223.

21 *Ibid.*, p. 156.

22 *Ibid.*

23 Trenner, *Die Skizzenbücher von Richard Strauss*, p. 6.

24 Strauss, *Betrachtungen und Erinnerungen*, p. 211.

25 Seidl, *Straussiana*, pp. 61–2.

26 Del Mar, *Richard Strauss*, vol. 1, p. 134.

27 Schmidt, *Aus dem Musikleben der Gegenwart*, p. 277; Schmalz, 'Richard Strauss' *Also sprach Zarathustra*', p. 121.

28 'On Poetry and Composition', *Richard Wagner's Prose Works*, vol. 6, p. 143.

29 Schmalz, 'Richard Strauss' *Also sprach Zarathustra*', p. 110.

30 Ludwig Schiedermair, cited in Herta Blaukopf (ed.), *Gustav Mahler-Richard Strauss: Correspondence 1888–1911*, trans. Edmund Jephcott (London: Faber, 1984), pp. 120–1.

4 Composition and first performances

1 Steinitzer, *Richard Strauss*, p. 75.

2 Schuh, *Richard Strauss*, p. 419; Erich H. Mueller von Asow, *Richard Strauss: Thematisches Verzeichnis*, vols. 1, p. 185 and 3, p. 1640; Franz Trenner, *Richard Strauss Werkverzeichnis*, p. 40.

3 Schuh, *Richard Strauss*, pp. 408, 419.

4 Letter of 12 July 1895, *Strauss-Schillings Briefwechsel*, p. 34.

5 Letter of 2 August 1895, *Strauss-Schillings Briefwechsel*, pp. 35–7.

6 Trenner, *Die Skizzenbücher von Richard Strauss*, p. 4.

7 Schuh, *Richard Strauss*, p. 419.

8 *Ibid.*

9 *Wagner-Strauss Briefwechsel*, pp. 221–3; the 'handsome behaviour' refers to Strauss's conducting of Ritter's *Sursum corda!* in Munich on 7 March.

10 *Strauss-Schillings Briefwechsel*, p. 43; Trenner, *Die Skizzenbücher von Richard Strauss*, p. 6.

11 Günter Brosche and Karl Dachs (eds.), *Richard Strauss: Autographen in München und Wien Verzeichnis*, p. 235.

12 *Strauss-Schillings Briefwechsel*, pp. 44–8.

13 Schuh, *Richard Strauss*, p. 420.

14 Trenner, *Die Skizzenbücher von Richard Strauss*, p. 3.

15 Franz Grasberger (ed.), *'Der Strom der Töne trug mich fort': Die Welt um Richard Strauss in Briefen*, pp. 95–6.

16 Dietrich Kämper (ed.), *Richard Strauss und Franz Wüllner im Briefwechsel*, p. 32.

17 *Ibid.; Die Welt um Richard Strauss in Briefen*, p. 95.

18 *Strauss-Wüllner Briefwechsel*, p. 33.
19 *Ibid.*; Brosche and Dachs, *Richard Strauss: Autographen*, p. 236.
20 *Strauss-Wüllner Briefwechsel*, pp. 34–5.
21 Brosche and Dachs, *Richard Strauss: Autographen*, pp. 235–6.
22 Letter of 24 February 1899, *Strauss-Schillings Briefwechsel*, p. 55; letter to Spitzweg, July [?] 1897, Brosche and Dachs, *Richard Strauss: Autographen*, p. 140; see also Friedrich von Schuch, *Richard Strauss, Ernst von Schuch und Dresdens Oper*, pp. 15–16.
23 *Strauss-Schillings Briefwechsel*, pp. 56, 192–5; Schlötterer, 'Richard Strauss und sein Münchner Kreis', p. 21; see Mueller von Asow, *Richard Strauss: Thematisches Verzeichnis*, vol. 1, p. 186 for the various piano arrangements of *Also sprach Zarathustra*. The version for two hands was the work of Karl Schmalz, who subsequently wrote an article on the work; there was also a version for 'Salon- und kleines Orchester' by Arnold Wilke in what Universal described as its 'Vindabona-Collection'.

5 Reception

1   *Strauss: Briefe an die Eltern*, p. 201.
2   Brosche and Dachs, *Richard Strauss: Autographen*, pp. 237–8.
3   *Strauss: Briefe an die Eltern*, pp. 212–13.
4   See letter of 3 February 1899, *Strauss-Thuille Briefwechsel*, p. 153, for Thuille's congratulations after a performance in Paris on 22 January; see Schuh, *Richard Strauss*, p. 422, for Strauss's enthusiastic reaction to the *Generalprobe* in Frankfurt.
5   Franz Grasberger, *Richard Strauss und die Wiener Oper*, p. 13.
6   Eduard Hanslick, *Am Ende des Jahrhunderts*, pp. 265–71.
7   Hanslick seems to forget that Beethoven's symphony is noted for inclusion of trombones for the first time in the history of the genre.
8   Schuh, *Richard Strauss*, p. 380.
9   Steinitzer, *Richard Strauss*, pp. 227, 234.
10 Richard Specht, *Richard Strauss und sein Werk*, vol. 1, pp. 235–6.
11 *Ibid.*, vol. 1, p. 233.
12 Letters of 29 November 1899, 30 October 1901 and 3 November 1901, *Wagner-Strauss Briefwechsel*, pp. 236–7, 243–5.
13 Specht, *Richard Strauss*, vol. 1, p. 237; see Fritz Gysi, *Richard Strauss*, p. 55, for a rejection of Specht's opinion.
14 Hausegger, *Gedanken eines Schauenden*, p. 261.
15 Oscar Bie, *Die neuere Musik bis Richard Strauss*, p. 50.
16 E.g., Reinhold C. Muschler, *Richard Strauss*, pp. 23 and 329–30.
17 Specht, *Richard Strauss*, vol. 1, pp. 247–8; Batka, *Richard Strauss*, p. 15.
18 Steinitzer, *Richard Strauss*, pp. 234–5.
19 Grasberger and Hadamowsky, *Richard-Strauss-Ausstellung zum 100. Geburtstag*, p. 127.
20 Mendl, 'The art of the symphonic poem', pp. 452–5.
21 Otto Klauwell, *Geschichte der Programmusik*, p. 221.
22 *Ibid.*, p. 249.
23 *Ibid.*, pp. 257–8.
24 Dahlhaus, *Nineteenth-Century Music*, p. 361.
25 See, for instance, Strauss's characterization of the harp glissando in the first movement of Liszt's *Dante Symphony* as 'symbol' for the emergence of Francesca da Rimini and her lover from Hell, in Hector Berlioz, *Instrumentationslehre*, ed. Richard Strauss (2 vols., Leipzig: Peters, n.d. [1905]), vol. 1, p. 123.
26 Paul Moos, *Die Philosophie der Musik von Kant bis Eduard von Hartmann* (2nd edn, Berlin/ Leipzig: Deutsche Verlags-Anstalt and Schuster & Loeffler, 1922), pp. 465–75.
27 Herwarth Walden (ed.), *Richard Strauss: Symphonien und Tondichtungen*, pp. viii–ix.

28 Bie, *Die neuere Musik bis Richard Strauss*, pp. 35–6 and 49.
29 Jacques Barzun, 'The meaning of meaning in music: Berlioz once more', *Musical Quarterly*, 66 (1980), pp. 1–20.
30 Schuh, *Richard Strauss*, pp. 471–2.
31 See, for instance, Hans Merian, *Richard Strauss' Tondichtung 'Also sprach Zarathustra'*, pp. 10–13; Reinhard Gerlach, *Don Juan und Rosenkavalier*, p. 71.
32 Ernst Krause, *Richard Strauss: The Man and his Work*, pp. 44, 163, 216, 242–3.
33 *Die Welt um Richard Strauss in Briefen*, p. 105.
34 *Debussy on Music*, collected by François Lesure, trans. and ed. Richard Langham Smith (London: Secker and Warburg, 1977), p. 161.
35 Myers (ed.), *Richard Strauss and Romain Rolland*, p. 111.
36 *Ibid.*, pp. 111–12.
37 *Ibid.*, pp. 112, 122.
38 *Ibid.*, p. 134.
39 *Ibid.*, p. 114.
40 *Ibid.*, p. 162.
41 *Ibid.*, p. 177.
42 *Ibid.*, p. 191.
43 Michael Kennedy, *Strauss Tone Poems*, p. 30; Barbara Tuchman, *The Proud Tower: A Portrait of the World Before the War 1890–1914* (London: Hamish Hamilton, 1966), chapter 6, *passim*. Tuchman was a popular historian of great gifts, and the author of several very fine books, but when the subject is Germany and the Germans, she shows too great a willingness at times to resort to stereotyped national characteristics as a substitute for analysis of motivation.
44 Del Mar, *Richard Strauss*, vol. 1, p. 145.
45 Henry George Farmer, 'Nietzsche and Strauss', p. 244; Peter R. Franklin, 'Strauss and Nietzsche: a revaluation of *Zarathustra*', pp. 248–53.
46 Josef Rufer, *Composition with Twelve Notes*, p. 17.
47 Béla Bartók, *Essays*, ed. Benjamin Suchoff (London: Faber, 1976), p. 409.
48 Béla Bartók, *Letters*, ed. János Demény, trans. Péter Balabán and István Farkas (London: Faber, 1971), pp. 48, 50.
49 Graham Donald Bruce, *Bernard Herrmann: Film Music and Narrative* (Ann Arbor: UMI, 1985), p. 28.
50 Kennedy, *Strauss Tone Poems*, p. 34.
51 See David E. James, *Allegories of Cinema: American Film in the Sixties* (Princeton: Princeton University Press, 1989), pp. 12–13.
52 Hanslick, *Am Ende des Jahrhunderts*, p. 268.
53 Mark Audus, 'Krauss, Strauss and Vienna', sleevenote for the recording of *Also sprach Zarathustra* and *Don Quixote*, Decca CD 425 974–2 DM, 1990, 5.
54 Kennedy, *Strauss Tone Poems*, p. 34.

6 Narratives

1 Jean-Jacques Nattiez, 'Can one speak of narrativity in music?', *Journal of the Royal Musical Association*, 115 (1990), p. 244.
2 Roland Tenschert, *3×7 Variationen über das Thema Richard Strauss*, p. 38.
3 Arthur Hahn, cited in its reprinted form in Herwarth Walden (ed.), *Richard Strauss: Symphonien und Tondichtungen*, p. 125.
4 Del Mar, *Richard Strauss*, vol. 1, p. 143; Myers, *Richard Strauss and Romain Rolland*, pp. 186–7.
5 See Specht, *Richard Strauss und sein Werk*, vol. 1, p. 245, and Tenschert, *3×7 Variationen*, p. 38; Klauwell (*Geschichte der Programmusik*, p. 256) adds a further degree of confusion when he assumes that the 'Nachtwandlerlied' is 'Das andere Tanzlied'.
6 See Muschler, *Richard Strauss*, p. 333.

7 Del Mar, *Richard Strauss*, vol. 1, p. 144.
8 Lampert, *Nietzsche's Teaching*, p. 356; Friedrich Nietzsche, *Werke: Kritische Gesamtausgabe*, ed. Giorgio Colli and Mazzino Montinari (15 vols., Berlin: Walter de Gruyter, 1968), Part 6, vol. 1, p. 391.
9 E.g., Muschler, *Richard Strauss*, p. 97.
10 Mueller von Asow, *Richard Strauss: Thematisches Verzeichnis*, vol. 1, p. 188.
11 Del Mar, *Richard Strauss*, vol. 1, p. 136; Del Mar's disagreement with Specht (*Richard Strauss und sein Werk*, vol. 1, p. 240) over Strauss's intentions in quoting religious chant does not seem to affect their descriptions of the main A♭ song-theme.
12 See Roger Hollinrake, *Nietzsche, Wagner, and the Philosophy of Pessimism* (London: George Allen and Unwin, 1982), chapter 12; see also the introduction to *Thus Spoke Zarathustra: A Book for Everyone and No One*, trans. R. J. Hollingdale, pp. 34–5. Lampert (*Nietzsche's Teaching*, p. 355) suggests a number of significant modifications to Hollinrake's view of the character of the Sorcerer.
13 Tenschert, *3×7 Variationen*, p. 180.
14 Lampert, *Nietzsche's Teaching*, pp. 234–5.
15 I disagree, therefore, with Specht's comment (*Richard Strauss und sein Werk*, vol. 1, pp. 247–8) that book and tone poem are particularly far apart in 'Der Genesende'.
16 All references to Hahn's pamphlet are to Walden, *Richard Strauss: Symphonien und Tondichtungen*, pp. 109–27.
17 Walden, *Richard Strauss: Symphonien und Tondichtungen*, p. 109; Gustav Brecher also connected the figures of Zarathustra and Faust in a monograph approved by the composer (*Richard Strauss*, pp. 31–2).
18 Schuh, *Richard Strauss*, p. 421; the reference here is surely not to Arthur Seidl, who did, however, write an essay on *Also sprach Zarathustra* ('Also sang Zarathustra', contained in *Moderner Geist in der deutschen Tonkunst*, pp. 82–117), but to Arthur Hahn, since the latter's publisher was Bechhold. If Schuh is in error, then the mistake is reproduced by Kennedy (*Strauss Tone Poems*, p. 32).
19 For the cock-crow, see Specht, *Richard Strauss und sein Werk*, vol. 1, p. 243; Schmalz, 'Richard Strauss' *Also sprach Zarathustra*', p. 107; Otto Erhardt, *Richard Strauss: Leben, Wirken, Schaffen*, p. 137.
20 Seidl, *Moderner Geist in der deutschen Tonkunst*, p. 91.
21 Del Mar, *Richard Strauss*, vol. 1, p. 142.
22 Klauwell, *Geschichte der Programmusik*, p. 253.
23 *Gedanken eines Schauenden*, pp. 249–51.
24 Franklin, 'Strauss and Nietzsche', p. 249; Seidl, *Moderner Geist in der deutschen Tonkunst*, p. 95.
25 Franklin's later comments on the hero in Strauss suggest that he has not changed his opinion of this; see *The Idea of Music*, p. 34.
26 Franklin, 'Strauss and Nietzsche', pp. 249–51.
27 *Ibid.*, p. 252.
28 Specht, *Richard Strauss und sein Werk*, vol. 1, pp. 231–3; Franklin, 'Strauss and Nietzsche', p. 253; Kennedy, *Strauss Tone Poems*, p. 34.

7 Structures

1 Batka (*Richard Strauss*, pp. 15–16) argues essentially for an expressive intention.
2 Reinhard Gerlach, *Don Juan und Rosenkavalier*, pp. 74, 77.
3 E.g., in George Perle, *The Operas of Alban Berg* (2 vols., Berkeley: University of California, 1980–5), *passim*.
4 Schmalz, 'Richard Strauss' *Also sprach Zarathustra*', p. 112.
5 Arno Forchert, 'Techniken motivisch-thematischer Arbeit in Werken von Strauss und Mahler', pp. 191–94.

6 Hans Merian, *Richard Strauss' Tondichtung 'Also sprach Zarathustra'*, pp. 10–13.
7 Derrick Puffett, *Richard Strauss: 'Salome'*, pp. 65–6.
8 Merian, *Richard Strauss' Tondichtung 'Also sprach Zarathustra'*, pp. 16–21.
9 Specht, *Richard Strauss und sein Werk*, vol. 1, p. 241.
10 Tethys Carpenter, 'Tonal and dramatic structure', in Puffett, *Richard Strauss: 'Salome'*, p. 88.
11 Merian, *Richard Strauss' Tondichtung 'Also sprach Zarathustra'*, pp. 24–5, 54.
12 Lorenz, 'Der formale Schwung in Richard Strauss' *Till Eulenspiegel*', p. 668.
13 Tenschert, *3×7 Variationen*, p. 38.
14 Steinitzer, *Richard Strauss*, pp. 236–7.
15 *Ibid.*, pp. 234–5.
16 Theodor W. Adorno, *Mahler: Eine musikalische Physiognomik* (Frankfurt a.M.: Suhrkamp, 1960).
17 Arno Forchert, 'Zur Auflösung traditioneller Formkategorien in der Musik um 1900', pp. 93–7; an extreme statement of this approach is provided by Wolfgang Dömling (cited by Forchert), that Strauss made use of 'the trivial nineteenth-century literary interpretation of music' as 'composed-out hermeneutics'.
18 Dahlhaus, *Nineteenth-Century Music*, p. 363.
19 Gerlach, *Don Juan und Rosenkavalier*, p. 71.
20 Edward Murphy, 'Tonal organization in five Strauss tone poems', pp. 230–1.
21 See Lina Ramann, *Franz Liszt als Künstler und Mensch* (2 vols., Leipzig: Breitkopf und Härtel, 1880–94), vol. 2, p. 152; see also John Williamson, 'The Revision of Liszt's *Prometheus*', *Music & Letters*, 67 (1986), p. 381.
22 Specht, *Richard Strauss und sein Werk*, vol. 1, p. 243; Murphy, 'Tonal organization in five Strauss tone poems', pp. 230–1.
23 Specht, *Richard Strauss und sein Werk*, vol. 1, p. 244; Wilde, *The Development of Melody in the Tone Poems of Richard Strauss*, p. 179.
24 Fuller consideration of these transformations can be found in Wilde, *The Development of Melody in the Tone Poems of Richard Strauss*, pp. 181–90.
25 Schuh, *Richard Strauss*, p. 486.
26 Waltershausen, *Richard Strauss*, p. 66.
27 Merian, *Richard Strauss' Tondichtung 'Also sprach Zarathustra'*, p. 16; Wilde, *The Development of Melody in the Tone Poems of Richard Strauss*, pp. 158, 179; Gerlach, *Don Juan und Rosenkavalier*, p. 72; Del Mar, *Richard Strauss*, vol. 1, p. 146.
28 Walter Schrenk, *Richard Strauss und die neue Musik*, p. 77; Fritz Gysi, *Richard Strauss*, p. 55.
29 Muschler, *Richard Strauss*, p. 327.
30 Adorno, *Mahler*, p. 116.
31 Walter Frisch, *Brahms and the Principle of Developing Variation* (Berkeley: University of California, 1984), p. 49.
32 Wilde, *The Development of Melody in the Tone Poems of Richard Strauss*, p. 194.
33 Dahlhaus, *Klassische und romantische Musikästhetik*, p. 388.

8 Rhetoric

1 Leonard G. Ratner, *Classic Music: Expression, Form, and Style*, p. 31.
2 Ernst Kurth, *Romantische Harmonik*, pp. 118, 191, 258, 304, 362.
3 Lee A. Rothfarb, *Ernst Kurth as Theorist and Analyst*, p. 190.
4 Ernst Kurth, *Bruckner* (2 vols., Berlin: Max Hesses Verlag, 1925; *R* Hildesheim: Georg Olms, 1971), vol. 1, pp. 364–5.
5 Schuh, *Richard Strauss*, p. 419.
6 Graham H. Phipps, 'The logic of tonality in Strauss's *Don Quixote*', pp. 189–205 (see in particular p. 191).
7 Arnold Schoenberg, *Structural Functions of Harmony*, p. 20.

8 *Ibid.*, chapter 9.

9 Ernö Lendvai, *The Workshop of Bartók and Kodály* (Budapest: Editio Musica Budapest, 1983), pp. 269–317.

10 Arnold Schoenberg, *Theory of Harmony*, p. 366; Lendvai, *The Workshop of Bartók and Kodály*, pp. 276–7.

11 Murphy, 'Tonal organization in five Strauss tone poems', pp. 230–1.

12 Schoenberg, *Theory of Harmony*, pp. 128, 383–4.

13 See Robert W. Wason, *Viennese Harmonic Theory from Albrechtsberger to Schenker and Schoenberg* (Ann Arbor: UMI, 1985), p. 46.

14 Rothfarb, *Ernst Kurth*, pp. 114, 184.

15 Rudolf Louis and Ludwig Thuille, *Harmonielehre*, pp. 382–3.

16 Schoenberg, *Theory of Harmony*, p. 384.

17 See above, pp. 34–5.

18 Natalie Bauer-Lechner, *Recollections of Gustav Mahler*, trans. Dika Newlin, ed. Peter Franklin (London: Faber, 1980), p. 173.

19 Ratner, *Classic Music*, p. 83.

9 Afterword

1 *Die Welt um Richard Strauss in Briefen*, p. 436.

2 Schuh, *Richard Strauss*, p. 420.

3 *The Correspondence between Strauss and Hofmannsthal*, p. 404.

4 Kenneth Birkin, *'Friedenstag' and 'Daphne'*, pp. 210–17, 230–3.

5 Del Mar, *Richard Strauss*, vol. 1, pp. 145–6.

6 Trenner, *Die Skizzenbücher von Richard Strauss*, pp. 18–19, 26–7, 31–2, 35–40, 43–4, 47–8. I am grateful to Dr Eveline Nikkels for access to her unpublished paper, 'Mahler und Strauss und ihre Beziehungen zu der Philosophie von F. Nietzsche', which discusses some of these annotations.

Bibliography

Batka, Richard. *Richard Strauss* (Charlottenburg: Virgil, n.d. [1908])

Bie, Oscar. *Die neuere Musik bis Richard Strauss* (*Die Musik*, vols. 33–4; Leipzig: Kistner und Siegel, n.d. [1925])

Birkin, Kenneth. *'Friedenstag' and 'Daphne': An Interpretive Study of the Literary and Dramatic Sources of Two Operas by Richard Strauss* (New York and London: Garland, 1989)

Botstiber, Hugo. *Geschichte der Ouvertüre und der freien Orchesterformen* (Leipzig: Breitkopf & Härtel, 1913)

Brecher, Gustav. *Richard Strauss: Eine monographische Skizze* (Leipzig: H. Seemann Nachfolger, n.d. [1900])

Brosche, Günter, and Dachs, Karl (eds.). *Richard Strauss: Autographen in München und Wien Verzeichnis* (Tutzing: Hans Schneider, 1979)

Dahlhaus, Carl. *Klassische und romantische Musikästhetik* (Laaber, 1988)

Nineteenth-Century Music, trans. J. Bradford Robinson (Berkeley: University of California, 1989)

Del Mar, Norman. *Richard Strauss: A Critical Commentary on his Life and Works* (3 vols., 2nd edn, London: Faber, 1986)

Eggebrecht, Hans Heinrich. 'Symphonische Dichtung', *Archiv für Musikwissenschaft*, 39 (1982), 223–33

Erhardt, Otto. *Richard Strauss: Leben, Wirken, Schaffen* (Olten/Freiburg: Otto Walter, 1953)

Farmer, Henry George. 'Nietzsche and Strauss', *Music Review*, 4 (1943), 243–9

Forchert, Arno. 'Zur Auflösung traditioneller Formkategorien in der Musik um 1900: Probleme formaler Organisation bei Mahler und Strauss', *Archiv für Musikwissenschaft*, 32 (1975), 85–98

'Techniken motivisch-thematischer Arbeit in Werken von Strauss und Mahler', *Hamburger Jahrbuch für Musikwissenschaft*, 2 (1977), 187–200

Franklin, Peter. 'Strauss and Nietzsche: a revaluation of *Zarathustra*', *Music Review*, 32 (1971), 248–53

The Idea of Music: Schoenberg and Others (London: Macmillan, 1985)

Gerlach, Reinhard. *Don Juan und Rosenkavalier: Studien zu Idee und Gestalt einer tonalen Evolution im Werk Richard Strauss'* (Bern: Paul Haupt, 1966)

Grasberger, Franz (ed.). *'Der Strom der Töne trug mich fort': Die Welt um Richard Strauss in Briefen* (Tutzing: Hans Schneider, 1967)
Richard Strauss und die Wiener Oper (Tutzing: Hans Schneider, 1969)
and Hadamowsky, Franz (eds.). *Richard-Strauss-Ausstellung zum 100. Geburtstag* (Vienna: Österreichische Nationalbibliothek, 1964)
Gregor, Joseph. *Richard Strauss: Der Meister der Oper* (Munich: Piper, 1939)
Gysi, Fritz. *Richard Strauss* (Potsdam: Akademische, 1934)
Hahn, Arthur. *Richard Strauss: 'Also sprach Zarathustra'* (Frankfurt a.M.: H. Bechhold, n.d. [1897?])
Hanslick, Eduard. *Am Ende des Jahrhunderts: Musikalische Kritiken und Schilderungen* (2nd edn, Berlin: Allgemeiner Verein für Deutsche Literatur, 1899; R Gregg International, 1971)
Hausegger, Friedrich von. *Die Musik als Ausdruck* (2nd edn, Vienna: C. Konegen, 1887)
Gedanken eines Schauenden: Gesammelte Aufsätze, ed. Siegmund von Hausegger (Munich: F. Bruckmann, 1903)
Kämper, Dietrich (ed.). *Richard Strauss und Franz Wüllner im Briefwechsel* (Cologne: Arno Volk, 1963)
Kennedy, Michael. *Richard Strauss* (London: Dent, 1976)
Strauss Tone Poems (London: BBC, 1984)
Klauwell, Otto. *Geschichte der Programmusik von ihren Anfangen bis zur Gegenwart* (Leipzig: Breitkopf & Härtel, 1910)
Krause, Ernst. *Richard Strauss: The Man and his Work*, trans. John Combs (London: Collet's, 1964)
Kurth, Ernst. *Romantische Harmonik und ihre Krise in Wagners 'Tristan'* (3rd edn, Berlin: Max Hesses Verlag, 1923)
Lampert, Laurence. *Nietzsche's Teaching: An Interpretation of 'Thus Spoke Zarathustra'* (New Haven and London: Yale, 1986)
Lorenz, Alfred. 'Der formale Schwung in Richard Strauss' *Till Eulenspiegel'*, *Die Musik*, 17 (1924/5), 658–69
Louis, Rudolf, and Thuille, Ludwig. *Harmonielehre* (8th edn, Stuttgart: Grüninger, n.d. [1924])
Mendl, R. W. S. 'The art of the symphonic poem', *Musical Quarterly*, 18 (1932), 443–62
Merian, Hans. *Richard Strauss' Tondichtung 'Also sprach Zarathustra': Eine Studie über die moderne Programmsymphonie* (Leipzig: Carl Meyers graphisches Institut, 1899)
Mueller von Asow, Erich H. *Richard Strauss: Thematisches Verzeichnis* (3 vols., Vienna/Wiesbaden/Munich: Doblinger, 1959–66)
Murphy, Edward. 'Tonal organization in five Strauss tone poems', *Music Review*, 44 (1983), 223–33
Muschler, Reinhold C. *Richard Strauss* (Hildesheim: Franz Borgmeyer, n.d. [1924])

Myers, Rollo (ed.). *Richard Strauss and Romain Rolland: Correspondence, Diary and Essays* (London: Calder and Boyars, 1968)

Newman, Ernest. *Richard Strauss* (London/New York: John Lane, 1908)

Nietzsche, Friedrich. *Thus Spoke Zarathustra: A Book for Everyone and No One*, trans. R. J. Hollingdale (rev. edn, Harmondsworth: Penguin, 1969)

Phipps, Graham H. 'The logic of tonality in Strauss's *Don Quixote*: a Schoenbergian evaluation', *19th Century Music*, 9 (1985/6), 189–205

Puffett, Derrick. *Richard Strauss: 'Salome'* (Cambridge: CUP, 1989)

Ratner, Leonard G. *Classic Music: Expression, Form, and Style* (New York: Schirmer, 1980)

Rothfarb, Lee A. *Ernst Kurth as Theorist and Analyst* (Philadelphia: University of Pennsylvania Press, 1988)

Rufer, Josef. *Composition with Twelve Notes Related Only to One Another*, trans. Humphrey Searle (5th rev. edn, London: Barry and Jenkins, 1970)

Schäfer, Theo. *Also sprach Richard Strauss zu mir: Aus dem Tagebuch eines Musikers und Schriftstellers* (Dortmund: Fr. Wilhelm Ruhfus, n.d. [1924])

Scherchen, Hermann. 'Das Tonalitätsprinzip und die Alpen-Symphonie von R. Strauss', *Melos*, 1 (1920), 198–204 and 244–6.

Schlötterer, Roswitha. 'Richard Strauss und sein Münchner Kreis', in *Jugendstil-Musik? Münchner Musikleben 1890–1918*, ed. Robert Münster and Hellmut Hell (Wiesbaden: Dr Ludwig Reichert, 1987)

(ed.). *Richard Strauss-Max von Schillings: Ein Briefwechsel* (Pfaffenhofen: W. Ludwig, 1987)

Schmalz, Karl. 'Richard Strauss' *Also sprach Zarathustra* und *Ein Heldenleben*: Ein Vergleich', *Die Musik*, 4 (1904/5), 102–23

Schmidt, Leopold. *Aus dem Musikleben der Gegenwart: Beiträge zur zeitgenössischen Kunstkritik* (Berlin: A. Hofmann, 1909)

Schoenberg, Arnold. *Structural Functions of Harmony*, ed. Leonard Stein (rev. edn, London: Faber, 1969)

Theory of Harmony, trans. Roy E. Carter (London: Faber, 1978)

Schrenk, Walter. *Richard Strauss und die neue Musik* (Berlin: Wegweiser, 1924)

Schuch, Friedrich von. *Richard Strauss, Ernst von Schuch und Dresdens Oper* (2nd edn, Leipzig: Verlag der Kunst, 1953)

Schuh, Willi (ed.). *Richard Strauss: Briefe an die Eltern 1882–1906* (Zurich and Freiburg: Atlantis, 1954)

Richard Strauss: A Chronicle of the Early Years 1864–1898, trans. Mary Whittall (Cambridge: CUP, 1982)

and Trenner, Franz (eds.). *Hans von Bülow and Richard Strauss: Correspondence*, trans. Anthony Gishford (London: Boosey & Hawkes, 1955)

Seidl, Arthur. *Moderner Geist in der deutschen Tonkunst* (Berlin: Harmonie, 1900; 2nd edn, Regensburg: Gustav Bosse, n.d. [1913])

Straussiana: Aufsätze zur Richard Strauss-Frage aus drei Jahrzehnten (Regensburg: Gustav Bosse, n.d. [1913])

Specht, Richard. *Richard Strauss und sein Werk* (2 vols., Leipzig/Vienna/Zurich: E. P. Tal, 1921)

Steinitzer, Max. *Richard Strauss* (Berlin and Leipzig: Schuster und Loeffler, 1911)

Strauss, Richard. *The Correspondence between Richard Strauss and Hugo von Hofmannsthal*, trans. Hans Hammelmann and Ewald Osers (Cambridge: CUP, 1980)

Betrachtungen und Erinnerungen (3rd edn, Zurich and Freiburg: Atlantis, 1981)

Tenschert, Roland. *3×7 Variationen über das Thema Richard Strauss* (Vienna: Wilhelm Frick, 1944)

Trenner, Franz (ed.). *Richard Strauss: Dokumente seines Lebens und Schaffens* (Munich: C. H. Beck, 1954)

Die Skizzenbücher von Richard Strauss aus dem Richard-Strauss-Archiv in Garmisch (Tutzing: Hans Schneider, 1977)

Cosima Wagner-Richard Strauss: Ein Briefwechsel (Tutzing: Hans Schneider, 1978)

Richard Strauss-Ludwig Thuille: Ein Briefwechsel (Tutzing: Hans Schneider, 1980)

Richard Strauss Werkverzeichnis (Vienna/Munich: Doblinger, 1985)

'Walden, Herwarth' [Georg Levin] (ed.). *Richard Strauss: Symphonien und Tondichtungen* (Berlin: Schlesinger, n.d. [1908?])

Waltershausen, Hermann W. von. *Richard Strauss: Ein Versuch* (Munich: Drei Masken, 1921)

Wilde, Denis. *The Development of Melody in the Tone Poems of Richard Strauss: Motif, Figure, and Theme* (Lewiston and Lampeter: Edwin Mellen, 1990)

Williamson, John. 'Strauss and *Macbeth*: the realisation of the poetic idea', *Soundings*, 13 (1985), 3–21

Index